**FROM ACONITE
TO THE ZODIAC KILLER**

A
Dictionary
of
Crime

AMANDA LEES

ROBINSON

ROBINSON

First published in Great Britain in 2020 by Robinson

A CIP catalogue record for this book is available from the British Library.

ISBN: 978-1-47214-329-7

Typeset in Sentinel Light by Hewer Text UK Ltd, Edinburgh
Printed and bound in Great Britain by Clays Ltd, Elcograf S.p.A.

Papers used by Robinson are from well-managed
forests and other responsible sources.

Robinson
An imprint of
Little, Brown Book Group
Carmelite House
50 Victoria Embankment
London EC4Y 0DZ

An Hachette UK Company
www.hachette.co.uk

www.littlebrown.co.uk

Amanda Lees was born in Hong Kong. She is the author of the bestselling satirical novels *Selling Out* and *Secret Admirer* (Pan) which have both received critical acclaim and have been translated into several languages. Her major YA thriller trilogy, *Kumari, Goddess of Gotham*, was nominated for the *Guardian* Children's Book Prize and the Doncaster Book Award. It also featured as Redhouse Book of The Month and Lovereading4kids Book of the Month. Amanda appears regularly on BBC radio and LBC and was a contracted writer to the hit series *Weekending* on Radio 4. She has written for, or contributed to, the *Evening Standard, The Times, New Woman, US Cosmopolitan* and Bulgaria's *Vagabond* magazine. Amanda has conducted a love coaching phone-in from the sofa of *Richard & Judy* and wooed the viewers on Channel 5 Live. She won an award at the Hungarian Győr Film Festival for a short film she produced, a psychological thriller called *Pros and Cons*.

For Delilah

Introduction

The crime bug bit me the day my father died although I didn't realise it until much later. I was only three at the time, so my memories are blurred but the hints my mother dropped over the years sharpened a different kind of focus. She would refer to the secretive work he had done and to the infamous spies he knew, usually after a sherry or three. Then there were the oblique mentions of his sudden, untimely death, his glamorous first wife and a mysterious fire that had burned down their London house. Mix in his Oxford education, murmurs of British intelligence and colonial missions lost in the mists of time, and the ramifications were obvious.

My dad was a spy and he had probably been murdered. Or he could still be alive somewhere, a prisoner or even a defector. Almost every kid who has lost a parent thinks they might secretly be alive. Not every kid has a writer's nose for a story or the tantalising details that could not be explained away. I used to scan faces at airports and wonder if one of them was my dad. I knew in my heart that he was dead, but I still picked at that murder theory. Yes, he probably did die of peritonitis, as I was told. But then again, you never know. You never know because people are far more complex than we think and, as I have learned, capable of anything.

It is that refusal to take anything at face value that has fuelled my fascination with crime and led me down many dark alleyways. Some existed only in my mind. Others were more physical. I spent my days at a Devonian convent boarding school devouring Agatha Christie, who was coincidentally born in Torquay, where my school was located. Christie loved a coincidence and I identified strongly with this woman who had developed her expertise in poisons after volunteering as a nurse during the war and assisting a hospital pharmacist.

I grew up in the Hong Kong hospital where my mother was matron, birth, death and everything in between providing the backdrop to my childhood. It was the same hospital where my father was apparently misdiagnosed and died. The hospital that I suspected, in my youthful imagination, of a cover up. Like Christie, I was intrigued by the power of substances to kill or cure. The Chinese have used potent herbs for thousands of years to do just that, as have monks and nuns since the Middle Ages. It was inevitable that I would want to tap into their horticultural legacy to spice up the stories I was already writing, the shadow of Christie falling over the pages I scrawled.

Later, I soaked up le Carré, P. D. James and every hard-boiled hack I could find before moving on to true crime, psychological thrillers and the cool, spare prose of Scandi noir. Spurning an English degree for drama, I learned to create a character and, more importantly, to dig for what motivated them. The play I wrote and directed for my finals centred on the abduction and murder of a child from a fairground and stunned the audience into silence. I took a first for that and the foundations of my future as a writer were laid. But first I was determined to act or rather act out what I thought was my father's life of adventure. I plunged into it headlong with often terrifying results.

On the Baltic cruise ship where I wrote and performed murder mysteries to entertain some of the world's richest and most ruthless people, I gazed at the palm of the ex-head of the KGB and imagined those same hands brutally torturing dissidents. Later, I knocked back rakia with Bulgarian Mafiosi and fended off a City fraudster who went on the run to escape prison for the millions he had embezzled.

A lowlight of my acting career was playing Catherine Eddowes, Jack the Ripper's fourth victim, for a Japanese TV film directed by a man who screamed constantly for more violence. One of my closest friends was a Metropolitan Police officer, a relative was a criminal barrister. I sat in the well of the Old Bailey as a bunch of old lags went down for one last botched hold-up to shouts of 'shame' from their families and watched police tapes that no one should ever have to see.

All that time I was doing what so many of us do when we read or watch true crime and crime fiction. I was trying to make sense of it and the way it touched my world. We crime lovers are voyeurs, but we are also hackers, driven to crack the code. We want to know how and why but we also want to know what we can do to protect ourselves. We want to help solve cold cases partly because we know it could happen to anyone. Yes, even to us. Especially to us.

That meeting with the ex-head of the KGB led, years later, to my taking on Putin's regime as part of a mission to save a dying man from prison. The man was chained to his bed in a Moscow cell, accused of crimes he did not commit. I used my skills as a writer to bolster the efforts of the lawyers who eventually won his release. The experience changed the direction of my writing, as did the simultaneous death of my mother. I returned to the darkness to which I had always been drawn, to write of the unspeakable things we can do to one another.

I had experienced evil at first hand. Now I wanted to make sense of it. I drew on my acting training to find the motives that drove my characters. Motive is one of the first things an investigator looks for when tackling a crime. Sometimes that motive seems irrational to everyone but the perpetrator. Those are the random crimes that hit the headlines and send ripples of fear through you and me. But hearing those stories does at least alert us to the possibility that anything can happen, that to stay safe we must consider the unthinkable. And that, I believe, is both the pull and the purpose of true crime and crime fiction.

We shudder at the gory details and sigh when a body is discovered. We stare at photos of the culprit and see the flat, blank sheen of evil in their eyes. Sometimes when we look in the mirror we think we catch a glimpse of that same sheen and we turn away. Other times we lie awake at night and listen to the creaks and sighs, wondering if it's our turn. All the while, one question throbs underneath our everyday thoughts. What if? What if someone snatched our child from the streets or a fairground? What if he really killed her? What if a dead father was alive, somewhere out there? What if it happens to me?

To control those thoughts, we seek answers in the pages of books, on our screens big and small, by listening to endless podcasts. Millions gather on forums and social media to solve cases the professionals have long consigned to a closed file. Mistakes are picked up and details pored over in a collective act of attempted closure. The unsolved is unsettling, the lazy cop or biased media more bad apples to chew over. Crime is so compelling because it brings out the best and worst in us. It frightens us to the core while setting us free.

Every time I brush hands with danger I feel more alive. Stupid maybe, but true of so many people. But I don't get my thrills bungee jumping or performing hardcore parkour. The danger is not so much physical as psychological. I knew the ex-head of the KGB had given up espionage for more profitable pastimes long before. The Bulgarian Mafiosi were too busy parading their arrogance along with their bellies to worry about a lowly writer. Those police tapes I watched were just that. Tapes. Someone else's story played out for me to watch.

Their stories, however, stay lodged in my memory. The unsavoury characters I have met leave their own taint. I am drawn to the rot and repelled by it, like some carrion beetle. I want to burrow deep in the filth so that I can extract from it redemption, but happy endings are rare when it comes to true crime and even the cosiest fiction leaves victims in its wake.

A crime thriller or mystery is both interactive and intensely intimate. We try to get inside the mind of the writer or protagonist so that we can solve the clues even as we anticipate the ending. It's a rush when we get it right. A gut punch when we're wrong. This is a visceral experience like no other and we can do it from the comfort of our living rooms. Often the characters are people just like us, except that something sinister has happened to them. They give us the chance to live vicariously, to flirt with danger. They allow us to exercise our minds and emotions in a way we may never experience in real life. Except that there is always the chance that we might. Which is why we keep getting back on the rollercoaster for another ride.

The high stakes counterbalance the humdrum chaos of our own lives, especially if that chaos is domestic. Female crime fans outnumber male by a significant percentage, partly because their own lives are so full and fragmented with multiple responsibilities. Crime fiction lends order, especially if it is a police procedural. More than that, it takes us out of the ordinary. Good and evil are clear cut. Underlying themes are biblical or mythical in proportion. Passion, revenge, mayhem and murder stir the blood in the most domestically dulled of veins.

I understand that need for a crime fix. I am also driven to supply it. I feed that supply through words, my favourite weapon. But I began to realise that the one barrier to crime fans was the thing they craved most, knowledge. If a reader or viewer does not understand a phrase or term used, then it adds friction to their experience. They cannot fully immerse themselves in the mystery or the solving of it and are therefore robbed of their full rush.

Crime readers are a discerning bunch. They thrive on fact and thorough research underpinning fiction. The blue line between true crime and crime fiction grows ever thinner as writers serve up stories with a palatable coating that barely disguises their roots in real life. Readers crave authenticity, but they don't want it to get in the way of a good plot. In trying to solve that problem like so many others, I came up with the idea of a crime dictionary, one that would not simply give definitions but also enough context and background to oil the wheels of the rollercoaster. With it in hand, crime fans can simply jump on and enjoy one hell of a ride. That, after all, is the reason we do it.

From Aconite to the Zodiac Killer: A Dictionary of Crime is the culmination of my own restless search for answers. I am as guilty as anyone of needing to impose order. In my case, it is through my love of story and words, two gifts my father bequeathed me. I no longer search for his face in crowds. But I will always wonder. What I did not want was for any fellow crime fan to be left wondering too. Which is why, with this dictionary, you can now stand at the shoulder of monsters unencumbered. This is your companion on the ride, the friend who holds your hand as you scream at the scary bits. Take it with you as you climb aboard. It is the best ride you will ever take.

A

AA
See **Air America**.

abbess
Bawd or bawdy woman who was the madame or mistress
of a brothel. A Covent Garden abbess was a procuress or
someone who procured customers for prostitutes. A Covent
Garden nun was a prostitute. Covent Garden in London
was once notorious for prostitutes and brothels and there
was no doubt competition for business, so the abbess had
an important job in drumming up business for her nuns.
The Covent Garden ague was a venereal disease often
contracted by customers of the Covent Garden nuns: 'He
broke his shins against the Covent Garden rails' was slang
meaning someone had contracted the venereal disease (UK
thieves' **cant**, historical slang).

ABFO scale
See **American Board of Forensic Odontology (ABFO)
scale**.

ABH
See **actual bodily harm**.

ABI
See **activity-based intelligence**.

absorbance

Absorbance is the measurement of how much light is absorbed by a substance. It is used within spectrophotometry on **trace evidence**. Also known as optical density.

abuse

Psychological, physical, sexual, financial or emotional mistreatment of a human being or other living creature by another person or persons. (See also **domestic assault**.) Also the illegal, improper or harmful use of something such as **alcohol** or **drugs**.

academy

Brothel. 'Floating academy' was the name given to brothels based on the floating prisons or 'hulks at Woolwich' for convicts (UK thieves' **cant**, historical slang).

access

In **intelligence** terms, a way to approach and identify a target or the ability to approach, or access, an individual, place or some information that enables the target to carry out the intended mission.

accessioning

Accessioning is the name given to the process of receiving, sorting, naming and labelling **forensic** samples. The specimen accessioner is the person who conducts this process and who is also responsible for allocating the samples to the correct departments for testing.

accessory before the fact

Someone who solicits or knowingly assists another person in the commission of a crime; often the person is not actually present at the time of the criminal act.

accessory to a crime

Someone who is involved in a crime, prior to or subsequent to its commission, but not present when it is actually carried out.

accomplice

Someone who knowingly plays a role in the perpetration of a crime in some way.

accusation

Statement that blames a specific person or persons for a criminal, illicit or illegal act.

accused

Someone **charged** with breaking the law. This is also used instead of the term 'defendant', which is not used in Scotland.

acint

See **acoustic intelligence**.

aconite (*Aconitum*)

Highly **poisonous** herbaceous perennial plant also known as monkshood, wolf's bane, devil's helmet and the queen of poisons. Aconite is fast-acting and, with large doses, death is almost instantaneous. Initial symptoms include nausea, vomiting and diarrhoea followed by burning, tingling and numbness in the mouth and burning in the abdomen. The main causes of death are paralysis of the heart and respiratory centres. The only post-mortem sign is of asphyxia leading to a common misdiagnosis of the cause of death as a heart attack. Despite the prevailing myth that it is undetectable, toxicology tests have existed for aconite for over two hundred years. It has featured as a murder weapon in the TV series *Midsomer Murders, Dexter* and *The Cadfael Chronicles* as well as in *American Horror Story* and James Joyce's *Ulysses*.

acoustic intelligence (acint)

Collection and processing of **intelligence** gained from listening devices, recordings and other acoustic phenomena.

acquittal

Verdict of a jury or decision of a judge that an **accused** is not guilty, or a **case** is not proven (the latter especially in Scotland).

acronym

An acronym is formed from the initial letters of other words and pronounced as a word. **Law enforcement** agencies and police forces worldwide use a variety of acronyms.

action

Working part of a **firearm** that **loads**, fires and ejects a **cartridge**. Lever, **pump** and **bolt actions** are found in weapons that fire a single shot. Firearms that can shoot multiple rounds, also known as repeaters, include all these types of actions but only the **semi-automatic** does not require manual operation between **rounds**. A **machine gun** has a truly **automatic** action. Also an old US **Mafia** term for illegal profits or the potential profit from racketeering.

activity-based intelligence (ABI)

Analysis of structured data from multiple **sources** to discover objects, relationships or behaviours by resolving significant activity.

actual bodily harm (ABH)

Assault causing actual bodily harm (ABH) is assault or
battery that causes actual physical harm to the victim,
which can include bruises, scratches and bitemarks as well
as more serious injuries. The perpetrator need not intend to
cause actual bodily harm but only to apply unlawful force to
the victim. ABH is a criminal offence under Section 47 of
the Offences Against the Person Act.

Adam

Accomplice (UK thieves' **cant**, historical slang).

Adam Tiler

Receiver of stolen goods, **fence** or **pickpocket** (UK
thieves' **cant**, historical slang).

addiction

State of physical and/or mental dependence on a **drug**,
including **alcohol** and **nicotine**, to such an extent that
stopping is immensely difficult and creates severe physical and mental trauma. Addiction is a recurring theme in
crime fiction and true crime and not always confined to
the perpetrators or victims. Addiction to drugs or alcohol
is often used to supply a detective such as Sherlock
Holmes or Jo Nesbø's Harry Hole with a humanising
flaw. Conan Doyle planted clues throughout the Holmes
series that point to his probable addiction to morphine
and cocaine. Irvine Welsh's DI Bruce Robertson in *Filth*
is a drug and sex addict as well as an alcoholic. The
fictional detectives Jane Tennison, Inspector Morse and
John Rebus are also alcoholics or borderline alcoholics

while Kathy Reich's Temperance Brennan, as befits her name, is an ex-alcoholic. In Paula Hawkins' thriller, *The Girl on a Train,* much of the action is seen through the blurred prism of the lead character, Rachel Watson, who often drinks until she blacks out.

A *British Medical Journal* study in 2013 quantified James Bond's consumption of alcohol and concluded that his weekly intake of 92 units a week was four times the recommended amount. At that rate, they calculated he would have died at the age of fifty-six. Some fictional detectives, such as Lawrence Block's Matt Scudder with his attendance at AA meetings, use their battle to maintain sobriety as a central pivot to their actions or to develop their character and story further, as Michael Brandman did when he took over the Jesse Stone series after the death of Robert B. Parker. Other characters are coloured by the experience of the authors, notably Raymond Chandler and Dashiell Hammett, who wrote at a time when a hard-drinking macho persona was preferable to the modern metrosexual who is more in touch with their feelings. Sue Grafton, author of the bestselling alphabetical detective series featuring PI Kinsey Millhone, acknowledged the effect her parents' alcoholism had on her writing and on the shaping of her protagonist, to whom she referred as her alter ego. James Lee Burke invented his character Dave Robicheaux in his own image as a recovering alcoholic. The flawed detective or **spy** may be a cliché or trope but it is one that is driven by the audience's appetite for figures with whom they can identify and who reflect the real-life addiction struggles of contemporary **law enforcement** officers as well as the readers themselves. ▶ **addictive** Causing addiction.

adjournment

Break in court proceedings, which can be for lunch, over-
night or for a longer period.

admissibility

Whether **evidence** is admissible. For evidence to be admitted in proceedings it must be reliable and relevant to a
factual issue in the **case**. Admissibility is always decided by
the trial judge.

Advanced Fingerprint Identification Technology (AFIT)

First used by the **Federal Bureau of Investigation** in
2011, AFIT implemented new matching algorithms to
increase accuracy in electronic automated **fingerprint**
identification.

affidavit

Written statement of **evidence** confirmed on oath or by
affirmation to be true and taken before someone who has
authority to administer it. This can sometimes be used in
court as witness evidence without the witness having to
come to court.

AFIS

See **Automated Fingerprint Identification System**.

AFIT

See **Advanced Fingerprint Identification Technology**.

agency

In **intelligence** terms, an individual or organisation that collects and/or processes information. Also known as a collection agency. ▶ **agent** Someone working for an **intelligence** service or agency, although the secret services usually refer to them as 'officers' rather than agents, with the **Federal Bureau of Investigation** being one exception. ▶ **agent of influence** Also known as a secret agent. A person in an influential position who uses that position to benefit the country or regime operating that agent. This can be through influencing public, cultural, scientific, intellectual and political opinion or decision making.

aggravated assault

An aggravated **assault** is a physical attack on another person that is aggravated by the use of a **deadly weapon**. It can also be considered aggravated if the intent was to cause serious harm to the victim or if injuries inflicted were serious.

AI

See **artificial intelligence**.

Air America (AA)

The US government owned and ran Air America as a passenger and cargo airline from 1950 to 1976, using it as a **cover** for military operations in areas where it could not otherwise operate. It was a dummy corporation for the **Central Intelligence Agency** and was later featured in a movie of the same name.

air gun

Gun that uses compressed air or gas to propel a **projectile**.

airsoft gun

Kind of **air gun** intended to look like a **firearm** and expelling small **pellets** such as plastic or aluminium **BBs**.

alcohol

Colourless, flammable liquid, produced by the fermentation of sugars, that forms the intoxicating element in wine, beer, cider, spirits and other drinks. It can also be used as a solvent, in fuel and in medicines. Used as a crutch or character flaw by detectives, to facilitate crimes and imbibed in legendary quantities by certain crime authors, including Raymond Chandler, Dashiell Hammett and Patricia Highsmith. Broads and booze are hallmarks of **hard-boiled crime fiction** while contemporary **thriller** writers such as Paula Hawkins create protagonists broken by the demon drink.

alias

Alternative or false name used to conceal a true identity.

alibi

Explanation, person or people that may prove a suspect was not at the scene of a crime when it happened.

all day

Serving a life **sentence** in prison– 'I'm doing all day' (US contemporary slang). ▶ **all day and a night** Serving a life sentence without **parole** (US contemporary slang).

allegation

Claim or **accusation** of a crime that has been made but not yet proved.

all points warning (APW)

Alert or description of a suspect or person of interest sent
out to airports, international train stations and ports to stop
them leaving the country (UK police acronym).

alternate light source

Also known as **forensic** light source. Powerful lamps used
in **crime scene investigations** that contain ultraviolet
(UV), visible and infrared components of light. The light is
filtered into individual colour bands or wavelengths that
help identify **evidence** through light interaction. UV light
is used primarily to identify **latent fingerprints** as well as
physiological fluids such as blood, semen and saliva
because these have natural fluorescent properties. Fibres,
shoeprints, human bone fragments, bitemarks and
gunshot residue are among the other applications.

Amber/AMBER alert

Alert sent out by police and **law enforcement** to ask for
the public's help when a child goes missing and is suspected
of having been abducted. Also known as a Child Abduction
Emergency alert (CAE). The term originated in the US
after ten-year-old Amber Hagerman was abducted and
killed in Texas in 1996 and is now used worldwide.

ambidexter

Lawyer who takes fees from both the plaintiff and the
defendant (UK thieves' **cant**, historical slang).

American Board of Forensic
Odontology (ABFO) scale

The ABFO scale is the US standard for measuring and
photographing bitemarks. The scale is L-shaped and

marked with circles and bars, to help compensate for camera-angle distortion and to determine exposure, as well as millimetres to aid measurement.

ammunition

Collective term for the material such as **bullets** that can be fired, dropped or **discharged** from a weapon.

amphetamine

Sold as a street **drug** as powder, pills or a paste, often wrapped in small pieces of paper referred to as wraps. Amphetamine (alpha-methylphenethylamine) is a **synthetic stimulant** that increases energy levels, confidence and alertness. It is the fourth most popular **illegal drug** in the UK. **Methamphetamine**, the stronger form of the drug commonly known as crystal meth because it usually comes in crystal form, is the second most popular illegal drug globally after **cannabis**. In the UK, most amphetamines are controlled as Class B drugs under the Misuse of Drugs Act. Methamphetamine is a Class A drug. The street and alternative names for amphetamine include: *acelerador*; Amy; amps; bam; b-bombs; beans; bennies; Benz; black and whites; black beauties; black birds; black bombers; black Mollies; blacks; blue boys; *bombita*; brain ticklers; brownies; bumblebees; cartwheels; chalk; chicken powder; chochos; chocolates; Christina; chunk; co-pilot; coast-to-coasts; crisscross; cross roads; cross tops; crosses; debs; dexies; diablos; diamonds; diet pills; dolls; dominoes; double cross; drivers; dulces; fives; flour; footballs; French blues; geeked up; goofballs; greenies; head drugs; hearts; horse heads; in-betweens; jelly babies; jelly beans; jolly beans; jugs; LA turnaround; leapers; lid poppers; lightening; little bombs; marathons; mini beans; mini bennies; morning shot; nuggets; oranges; pastas; pastillas; peaches; pep pills; pepper; pingas; pink hearts; pixies; pollutants; purple hearts; rhythm; rippers; road dope; roses; *rueda*; snaps; snow pallets; sparkle plenty; sparklers; speed; splash; sweeties; sweets; tens; thrusters; TR-6s; truck drivers; turnabouts; uppers; wake ups; West Coast turnarounds; wheels; whiffle dust; white crosses; whites; zoomers.

amphibious vehicle

Wheeled or tracked vehicle capable of operating on both land and water.

amuser

Thief who kept dust in their pockets to fling in the faces of their unsuspecting victims, robbing them while they were blinded and being followed by an **accomplice** who, on pretence of helping the victim, would take whatever was left (UK thieves' **cant**, historical slang).

amyl nitrite

Often confused with amyl nitrate but in fact a completely different substance. Amyl nitrite is a pale-yellow liquid used to open or widen blood vessels to allow more blood flow. Amyl nitrite was originally sold in small vials or capsules that had to be cracked or popped open, so the **drugs** became known as 'poppers'. Poppers are also known as liquid gold, butyl nitrite, heart medicine (from the original use of amyl nitrite in treating heart patients) and room deodoriser. It is often sold in small bottles and inhaled. Swallowing amyl nitrite is highly dangerous and can be fatal. It first became popular among the gay community as a recreational drug and to enhance the effects of sexual encounters as it results in an increased sex drive and heightened skin sensitivity as well as relaxing the walls of the anus and vagina. It is now used as a psychoactive drug by a wide range of people and clubbers in particular. People also take it for the rapid sense of euphoria it produces along with a temporary head **rush**. Poppers are legal to sell only as products that are not for human consumption. Possession in the UK is not illegal, but supply can be an offence.

analysis and production

In **intelligence** terms, converting processed information into intelligence through the integration, evaluation, analysis and interpretation of all **source** data and the preparation of finished intelligence products such as intelligence reports to meet known or anticipated user requirements.

▶ **analyst** An **intelligence analyst** acquires, evaluates, analyses and assesses information on behalf of the secret intelligence services, the military and the police.

angel of death/mercy

An angel of death or mercy is a caregiver or medical professional, usually a nurse, who deliberately harms or kills their patients, often justifying their actions to themselves by claiming to act out of mercy in the face of suffering. Others kill as a means of exerting sadistic power and control over their patients or to obtain money fraudulently from them while another variant, known as malignant heroes, deliberately harm patients so they can then by lionised by the victim's family for 'saving them'. Often serial killers, the typical medical professional who kills murders two patients a month, usually by **lethal** injection. Notorious examples include **Harold Shipman** and nurse Beverley Allitt whose **case** was dramatised in the BBC's *Angel of Death* (2005).

angler

This is a **thief** who specialises in breaking jewellers' display windows to steal the goods on display, often with a stick from which some kind of hook dangles in order to fish for the items. Also known as a hooker or starrer (UK thieves' **cant**, historical slang).

animal

Paedophile (UK contemporary prison slang).

ANPR

See **Automatic Number Plate Recognition**.

antemortem data

Medical records, samples and photographs taken prior to death. These include, but are not limited to, **fingerprints**, dental **X-rays**, body-tissue samples, and photographs of tattoos and other identifying marks. These records are compared to records completed after death to help establish a positive identification of human remains.

antimony

Antimony is a highly **toxic** metal that is found in many everyday items. It has been described as the perfect **poison** due to the fact it is odourless, colourless and near tasteless when dissolved, which means it is also easy to ingest without noticing. When inhaled antimony can cause symptoms that include headaches, dizziness, antimony spots on the skin, gastrointestinal upset, psychosis, convulsions and coma. Antimony also acts as a natural preservative, which means it may not be the perfect murder weapon unless the perpetrator also ensures the complete disposal of the corpse.

antique firearm

Firearm for which the year of model and/or manufacturing are considered as antique in national legislation. This definition excludes all firearms that can fire **ammunition**, or firearms that are prohibited or under authorisation. Antique guns manufactured before 1899 are not subject to import controls and are increasingly being used in gun crime to get around UK laws restricting access to **handguns**. The guns are modified, and ammunition imported or manufactured, often by street gangs using these weapons. Four such weapons have recently been linked to homicides in the UK, with 543 antique guns seized over the past decade. The UK government is therefore bringing in new laws to restrict the use of antique firearms.

antiterrorism

Defensive measures including physical items such as barriers and procedures used to reduce the vulnerability of individuals and property to terrorist acts.

appeal

Request by either the defence or the prosecution that a **case** be removed from a lower court to a higher court in order for a completed trial to be reviewed by the higher court. ▶ **appellant** Someone who lodges an **appeal**.

APW

See **all points warning**.

area damage control

Measures taken before, during and/or after an attack, natural or manmade disaster to reduce the likelihood of damage and minimise its effects.

area diving

Sneaking down steps and stealing from the lower rooms of a house (UK Victorian slang).

AR-15-style rifle

The AR-15-style **semi-automatic** lightweight **rifle** is used by **law enforcement** in the US and UK as well as other countries around the globe but has also been used in a number of mass shootings, including five of the ten deadliest mass shootings in American history. A Colt AR-15-style rifle was also used in the 1996 Port Arthur massacre in Australia, which led to restrictions on private ownership of semi-automatic weapons capable of firing more than five **rounds**, while the 2019 Christchurch mosque shootings in New Zealand resulted in a ban on semi-automatic weapons. The **Metropolitan Police Service** and other forces in the UK currently use the SIG Sauer SIG516 AR-15 variant.

ark ruffian

Villain who stole and sometimes murdered passengers on the water, often stripping them of all their goods before throwing them overboard. Ark ruffians would work in conjunction with the watermen (UK thieves' **cant**, historical slang).

arming

When applied to explosives, weapons and **ammunition**, the change from a safe state to a state of readiness for use.

arrest

Take a person into **custody** by restraint with the authority of law, for the purpose of charging them with a criminal offence terminating in the recording of a specific offence.

arrival zone

In anti-**drug** operations, the area in or adjacent to the country affected where the act of smuggling finishes and domestic distribution begins. This can be an airstrip in the case of smuggling by air or an offload or landing point if it is by sea.

arsenic

Beloved of crime writers from Agatha Christie to Dorothy L. Sayers, arsenic **poisoning** was a common murder method in Victorian Britain. The 1939 play and subsequent 1941 film of *Arsenic and Old Lace* were successful dark comedies that may have been inspired by the real-life serial killer and nursing-home owner, Amy Archer-Gilligan.

A notorious **case** in Scotland in 1857 centred on a young woman, Madeleine Smith, **charged** with murdering her lover, Pierre Émile L'Angelier, after he tried to blackmail her with their love letters when she ended the relationship. Although high quantities of arsenic were found in L'Angelier's stomach, Smith had been recorded buying arsenic from her local apothecary and L'Angelier's diary noted that he felt ill after drinking coffee and cocoa she served him, the case against Smith was found 'not proven'. It has been called the 'Crime of the Century' and causes debate among **forensic** scientists and criminologists to this day.

The Victorian fascination with the case reflected the fact this was the golden age of poisons, with arsenic a poison of choice because it was so readily available and, being tasteless and odourless, easy to conceal. Its effects could be explained away as food poisoning, as in the Smith case. Arsenic was such a popular poison and so easy to obtain that the Arsenic Act of 1851 was passed, requiring it to be dyed indigo.

Arsenic eating was fashionable in the nineteenth century as people believed it resulted in a clear complexion and healthy hair, and also that they could build up a tolerance to it by ingesting small quantities over a period of time. This theory was the plot premise in Dorothy L. Sayers' *Strong Poison* (1930), in which two people sit down to a dinner laced with arsenic and only one dies. In fact, science has since proved that humans generally only have a low tolerance to arsenic but that a genetic mutation can result in a much higher tolerance. This mutation is mainly found in populations where the drinking water has higher than normal levels of arsenic, such as in some remote regions of Chile, where scientists from the University of Santiago conducted their research, publishing their results in 2017. No doubt some enterprising author will incorporate this into a plot as poisoning is once more a fashionable murder method.

arson

The crime of arson occurs when a person deliberately and maliciously sets fire to property, including buildings, vehicles, boats and forests or land. A person who commits arson is known as an arsonist. Arsonists commonly use accelerants such as petrol or gasoline to start their fires, and the detection of such accelerants or the residue they leave is crucial in **forensic** fire **investigations**. One common reason to commit arson is to carry out an insurance **fraud**, although this is increasingly difficult as forensic detection methods become more advanced.

Armed Response Unit (ARU)

An Armed Response Unit is a team of armed police officers in the UK who are sent to tackle crimes being committed by armed criminals or those suspected of being armed. The team comprises police officers who have undergone specialist **firearms** and other training. They carry Glock 17 **pistols** as standard issue but may be armed with additional firearms as well as tasers. Armed officers also carry out royal protection duties as well as protecting government officials and visiting heads of state. Armed officers can hold the rank of specialist firearms officer (SFO), counter terrorist specialist firearms officer (CTSFO), Armed Response Vehicle officer (ARVO), Tactical Support Team officer (TSTO), close protection officer (CPO) and personal protection officer (PPO), authorised firearms officer (AFO) or rifle officer.

Armed Response Vehicle (ARV)

An Armed Response Vehicle is a UK police vehicle that transports authorised **firearms** officers along with their **lethal** and **non-lethal weapons**. As they are intended to be the **first responders** on a scene requiring armed officers, they are usually fast vehicles such as BMWs equipped with state-of-the-art satellite navigation systems.

artificial intelligence (AI)

Artificial intelligence, i.e. machine learning, including machines capable of emulating skills such as speech and facial recognition, is used by police and **intelligence** both in the UK and the US as well as other countries to aid **investigations** and operations, although its use is controversial with some officers expressing concerns over possible data bias. The National Data Analytics Solution (NDAS) project being run by the West Midlands Police includes a number of steps to ensure the programme is developed as ethically as possible, excluding anything related to ethnicity. In addition, NDAS is also consulting with various independent ethics groups and external experts. In California, Bay Area departments use software that relies on data collected from crime-victim reports, **arrests**, suspect histories and other pertinent data to predict when and where crime will occur. Tacoma, Washington, has seen a 22 per cent drop in residential burglaries as a result of using AI. Shot detection systems based on AI alert authorities in real time and provide specific information about the type of gunfire and where it originated. The systems have multiple sensors that pick up the sound of a gunshot then use a software algorithm to convert data into actionable intelligence. While the use of AI is rapidly increasing in **law enforcement** and crime detection, doubts about ethical considerations and its efficacy remain. In spite of those doubts, data-driven policing is here to stay.

ARU
See **Armed Response Unit**.

ARV
See **Armed Response Vehicle**.

Aryan Brotherhood
The Aryan Brotherhood aka the AB, the Brand, Alice Baker and One-Two, is a white supremacist US prison gang and **organised crime** syndicate with a fearsome reputation who operate a 'blood-in, blood-out' policy. You have to kill to get in and only get out when you're dead. Entry is by invitation only.

assault

Assault is generally defined in the UK as inflicting deliberate or reckless harm on another person. That harm can include physical and psychological harm. An assault is classified as an offence against a person, and there are varying degrees of assault including common assault, **actual bodily harm** (ABH) and **grievous bodily harm** (GBH).

assault rifle

Selective fire **rifle** with a detachable **magazine**. It is capable of firing in different modes (both fully **automatic** and **semi-automatic** fire) and is typically the standard infantry weapon in the armed forces.

asset

Source of information within a country or organisation for an officer or **spy** who is spying on that country or organisation. They are also sometimes referred to as **agents** or **informants**. Can also be an object or item that aids an **intelligence** operation. ▶ **asset validation** In **intelligence** terms, the process used to determine an **asset**'s authenticity, reliability, utility and suitability as well as the degree of control the **case officer** or others has over them.

assistant chief constable

Third highest rank of UK regional and special police forces, beneath **chief constable** and **deputy chief constable**. Its equivalent rank in the **Metropolitan Police Service** is **commander**.

assistant commissioner

'Assistant Commissioner of Police of the Metropolis' (AC) is the third highest rank within London's **Metropolitan**

A **Police Service** (MPS), ranking below **deputy commissioner** and above **deputy assistant commissioner**. It is considered equivalent to the role of chief constable in other British police forces.

associate

Someone who works with the **Mafia** but is not an official member of the organisation.

atropine

Atropine is extracted from the deadly nightshade plant, which is otherwise known as *Atropa belladonna*. Bitter-tasting, atropine works by disrupting the nervous system and symptoms of **poisoning** include a dry mouth, blurred vision, hallucinations, increased heart rate, coma and death. Atropine is not only a poison but an antidote against **nerve agents** such as **sarin** and pesticides as well as in the treatment of bradycardia (slow heart rate). It has been used in a number of murders, on one occasion administered as eye drops, and **attempted** murders, as well as in crime fiction, notably by Agatha Christie.

attempt

Act that is more than the planning of a crime and, due to its nature, is a substantial element of finally committing the crime. An attempt is a separate and distinct offence in and of itself, e.g. attempted murder or attempted **robbery**.

autem diver

Pickpocket who practised in churches; also church-warden or overseer of the poor who defrauded or deceived the parish, *autem* being a word for church (UK thieves' **cant**, historical slang).

authentication

This can be a security measure designed to protect a communications system from a fraudulent transmission by establishing the validity of a transmission or message or its originator. It can also be a means of identifying individuals and verifying their eligibility to receive specific categories of information as well as **evidence** by proper signature or seal that a document is genuine and official. In personnel recovery missions, authentication is the process whereby the identity of the person to be recovered is confirmed so that the rescuers can be sure they have the right individual.

Automated Fingerprint Identification System (AFIS)

Biometric computer system that allows **forensic examiners** to encode, digitise and search recovered **fingerprint** impressions against fingerprint record databases for identification purposes. **Advanced Fingerprint Identification Technology (AFIT)** replaced the **Federal Bureau of Investigation**'s AFIS segment of the **Integrated Automated Fingerprint Identification System** (IAFIS) in 2011 as part of the **Next Generation Identification** system.

automatic firearm

Any **firearm** that, once the first **round** has been fired, **loads** automatically and can, with each single pull of the **trigger**, fire a burst of many shots until the trigger is released (also known as a fully automatic firearm).

Automatic Number Plate Recognition (ANPR)

System that uses optical character recognition to read vehicle number plates and create vehicle location data. It does this through existing **CCTV** or road-rule enforcement cameras or with cameras dedicated to this task. It is used globally for **law enforcement** purposes and to check if a vehicle is licensed and/or insured.

autopsy

An autopsy is the medical examination of a corpse to determine the cause(s) of death or the extent of a disease.

away

In prison (UK contemporary and historical slang).

B

babysitter

Another name for a bodyguard, especially when used by the
security services.

back door

A back door is a hole deliberately left in a software program
to allow for updates. Back doors are also created by system
developers as shortcuts to speed access through security
during the development stage and are then forgotten and
never properly removed during final implementation.
Sometimes **hackers** and **crackers** will create their own
back door to a system by using a **virus** or a **Trojan** to set it
up, thereby allowing them future access at their leisure.
Hackers, crackers and bots exploit back doors for malicious
purposes and to carry out **cyberattacks**.

back-door parole

To die in prison (US contemporary slang).

backspatter pattern

Blood-spatter pattern resulting from blood drops that travel
in the opposite direction to the external force applied.
Associated with an entrance wound created by a
projectile.

backstop

Arrangements put in place to support the **cover** story and activities of an **agent** or officer so that their story will stand up if any enquires are made. These can include setting up documentary, technical, legal, monetary and other arrangements to make the cover story appear true.

bacon, bacon head

Paedophile – from rhyming slang, a 'bacon bonce' = a **nonce** (UK contemporary prison slang).

bag out

To draw a weapon (London contemporary gang slang associated with drill music).

bagging

Stabbed in the lower body (London contemporary gang slang associated with drill music).

bagman

Agent, person or officer who collects and distributes often illicit funds in the form of bribes and to pay **assets** and **spies**.

bail

Release of a defendant from **custody** until their next court appearance subject sometimes to financial security being given and/or compliance with specified conditions.

ballistics

Forensic ballistics is the examination of **evidence** relating to guns and **firearms** as well as the effect and behaviour of **projectiles** or exploding devices at a **crime scene**.

A forensic ballistics expert examines and matches fragments, **bullets** and other evidence to a suspect's weapon as well as examining probable trajectories to ascertain the location from where the weapon was fired. Examination of weapons and bullets can reveal characteristic marks including **rifling** or marks from a specific gun on a bullet. Examination of **propellants** can reveal chemical components. Ballistics studies can be used to examine any type of thrown or fired projectile. Ballistics is usually divided into three parts:

- Interior ballistics or the study of the projectile's movement inside the gun.
- Exterior ballistics or the study of the projectile's movement between the **muzzle** and the target.
- Terminal ballistics or the study of the projectile's movement and behaviour in the target.

bally, bali

Mask or balaclava (London contemporary gang slang associated with drill music).

Bamber

'Do a Bamber' is a police expression meaning to make a mistake, after the **case** of Jeremy Bamber who killed his adopted mother, father, sister and her children. He initially managed to place blame for the murders on his sister, Sheila Caffell, but then inadvertently revealed the truth to his girlfriend and was duly **sentenced** to life in prison (UK police slang).

bang out

Beat up (UK contemporary prison slang).

bang up

Lock in a **cell** or in prison (UK contemporary prison slang).

bar

Profession of **barrister**. The name is taken from the place counsellors and advocates stand in court, formerly separated from the rest of the courtroom by a bar. Lawyers are said to have been 'called to the bar' once they have qualified to be a barrister.

barker, barking iron

Gun, **pistol** or especially **revolver** used by a **thief** or **footpad** (UK thieves' **cant**, historical slang).

barrel

Cylindrical tube designed to contain the pressure of a **propellant** and direct the **projectile**. For many weapons it consists of a **chamber** ending a rifled or **smooth bore**. In a **revolver**, the barrel does not have a chamber.

barrister

Also known as a **brief** or counsel. A member of the bar, a lawyer entitled to represent clients in all the courts in England and Wales. In Scotland, an advocate performs the same role as a barrister.

basic

To be put on basic is to be confined to a **cell** with all privileges such as TV and books removed (UK contemporary prison slang).

Basic Command Unit (BCU)

In the new structure of the **Metropolitan Police** its previous thirty-two-borough model has been streamlined into twelve Basic Command Units, each made up of two or three boroughs. The rollout of these was completed in 2019.

basic intelligence

Fundamental material and facts about a location or situation that could be used to plan an **intelligence** or military operation and to evaluate subsequent information gathered.

batrachotoxin

A neurotoxin extracted from certain birds, beetles and the skin of several Central and South American frogs, including the golden dart frog, batrachotoxin is applied to the tips of the blow darts used by Colombian and other indigenous South American tribes. It acts on the heart muscles, causing arrythmia and cardiac arrest. One frog contains enough **poison** to kill ten men and there is no known antidote.

BAU

'Business As Usual' (UK police acronym).

bawd

Procuress or brothel keeper (UK thieves' **cant**, historical slang).

BB

BB guns are **air guns** that fire metallic steel **projectiles** the same size as BB birdshot, with a nominal diameter of .180 in. BB is also used to refer to air-weapon **ammunition** of .177 in (4.5 mm) diameter steel projectiles and also to the plastic BBs used in **airsoft guns**.

BCU

See **Basic Command Unit**.

beak

Magistrate or justice of the peace. To be 'up before the beak' means to be in court facing **charges** (UK thieves' **cant**, historical slang still in use).

beak hunting

Stealing poultry (UK Victorian slang).

beamer

Crack smoker (US/Jamaican contemporary gang slang).

bearer up

Person who robs someone who has been diverted or decoyed by a female **accomplice** (UK historical slang).

beast

Paedophile (UK contemporary prison slang); police (US/Jamaican contemporary gang slang).

beef

Criminal **charge** – 'I caught a **burglary** beef' (US contemporary slang); to have a problem with someone else – 'I had a beef with him so I shot him' (US and UK contemporary slang).

behavioural analysis

In criminal **investigations**, the analysis of offenders and the way in which they behave in committing a crime. Specialist units include the Behavioral Analysis Unit (BAU) of the **Federal Bureau of Investigation** National Center for the Analysis of Violent Crime (NCAVC).

bell

Bullet (London contemporary gang slang associated with drill music).

bench warrant

Warrant issued by a judge for an absent defendant to be **arrested** and brought before a court.

bend up

To restrain or confine a prisoner in their **cell** before moving them (UK contemporary prison slang).

Bess, Betty

Lockpick (UK thieves' **cant**, historical slang).

best evidence policy

Forensic laboratory policy that some items will not be examined based on the results of other testing, or due to other factors such as the manner of collection, **degradation** or limitations of the science.

bifurcation

Point in a **fingerprint** where a friction ridge divides or splits to form two ridges.

bigot case

Investigation into an area or subject matter so **sensitive** that it has to be handled on a need-to-know basis. Due to this sensitivity, access to the investigation is limited to personnel who have been cleared and listed on a 'bigot list'.

big red key

The 'big red key', also known as 'the enforcer', is a type of battering ram used to break down doors in the course of police raids and operations (UK police slang).

bilateral operation (bilat)

Operation jointly run between two **intelligence** agencies from either the same or different countries.

bilk

Swindle or cheat (UK thieves' **cant**, historical slang).

Bill

Police, also known as the Old Bill. *The Bill* was also a police show that ran on British TV from 1984 to 2010 (UK contemporary slang).

bindle paper

Clean sheet of paper that is folded in a specific manner and used to collect **evidence**, typically **trace evidence** such as hair, dust, paint chips or other tiny particles that are light and therefore easily lost. It often forms part of a trace evidence kit.

bind over for sentence

Order that requires the defendant to return to court on an unspecified date for sentencing.

BINGO seat

Seat at the back of the police car, supposedly where the laziest officer sits – BINGO stands for 'Bollocks I'm Not Getting Out' (UK police slang).

binky

Homemade syringe, usually created from an eyedropper, pen shaft and guitar string, for shooting up **drugs** (US contemporary prison slang).

biohazard bag

Plastic or paper bag specifically used to safely transport **evidence** samples from a crime or accident scene to another site, typically a laboratory. Biohazard bags prevent **contamination** of the evidence and also protect the handler from any harm presented by the samples.

biological agent

Microorganism, or a toxin derived from it, that can be used as a weapon in biological warfare, causing disease in people, plants or animals, or causing the degradation or destruction of material. ▶**biological weapon** Biological agents used to cause disease to threaten or destroy human life. These can include bacteria, toxins, fungi and viruses. The use of biological weapons in modern warfare is a war crime. Biological weapons are a staple of fiction, TV and film.

biological fluid

Fluid that originates from a human or animal. The most typical biological fluids found at a **crime scene** are blood, saliva, semen, vaginal fluid, urine and perspiration.

biological hazard

Organism, or substance derived from an organism, that can damage human or animal health.

biological material

Material that has a human or animal origin, most commonly encountered at **crime scenes**, e.g. blood, saliva, semen, skin cells.

biometrics

Measurement and analysis of unique human biological and behavioural characteristics. Often used to secure entry access or data with biological information such as **fingerprint** or iris recognition. ▶ **biometric characteristic** Also known as a biometric attribute or simply as a biometric. The biological and behavioural characteristic of an individual from which distinguishing, repeatable biometric features can be extracted for the purpose of recognition.

bird

Time in prison. Bird is derived from rhyming slang as birdlime = time, so 'doing bird' = spending time in prison (UK contemporary prison slang).

biscuit

Gun (US contemporary gang slang).

bitemark identification

Forensic odontologists use specific marks and patterns to identify a suspect from a bitemark on a victim. The practice first became accepted in 1974 in the US after a bitemark on the nose of an elderly murder victim was used to identify her killer, but it has recently been the subject of controversy and scientific scrutiny. There have to date been thirty-one exonerations in the US after **cases** based on bitemark **evidence** were re-examined and this has led to questions being raised over the validity of such evidence, which may result in it being banned.

bitt

Money (UK thieves' **cant**, historical slang). ▶**bitt or bit faker** Counterfeiter of coins (UK thieves' **cant**, historical slang). ▶**bitt queer** Counterfeit money (UK thieves' **cant**, historical slang).

blab

To inform or reveal secrets or the details of a criminal operation or plot (UK thieves' **cant**, historical and contemporary slang).

black

When used by **intelligence** or military services, black means being free of any hostile **surveillance**. Going black in **tradecraft** jargon means ensuring freedom from such surveillance before engaging in an operation or act connected to an operation. Can also mean **clandestine** or **covert**, especially when used by the **Central Intelligence Agency**, or being in an undetected or unknown location. Also blackmail (UK cockney historical slang). ▶**black operations (ops)** Covert or clandestine operations carried out by governments, military and private organisations that are not officially authorised and are deniable by the agencies that have instigated them.

black-bag job

Federal Bureau of Investigation version of breaking and entering. Gaining **covert** entry into residences or other buildings for the purposes of **intelligence** gathering. Often used to obtain files and other documents relating to **foreign intelligence agents** operating on US soil. Can also entail installing wiretaps and planting microphones without a warrant.

black hat

Cracker who exploits vulnerabilities in computer systems for illicit purposes. Black hats often share information with other black-hat crackers so they can exploit the same vulnerabilities before the victim becomes aware and takes appropriate measures. Can also refer to all kinds of illicit or illegal computer or internet activity.

Black List

When used by the **intelligence** or military services this is a list of individuals and their locations who are known or suspected to be hostile and whose capture and detention is a priority. (See also **Grey List** and **White List**.)

black powder

Earliest known form of **gunpowder**, which was invented over a thousand years ago and consists of nitrate, charcoal and sulphur.

black propaganda

Untraceable disinformation that is deniable by its source.

black rat

Originally a **Metropolitan Police** traffic officer but can now refer to all police officers (UK police slang).

Black Rover

Police warrant card when it is used to obtain free travel on a bus, tube or train.

black swan event

Occurrence so rare and with such an extreme impact that it could only have been predicted in retrospect.

Blackwater

American private military company founded by ex-Navy SEAL Erik Prince. It was renamed Xe Services in 2009 and Academi in 2011.

black widow

Derived from the name of the spider who kills her mate after mating, a black widow killer is a woman who kills her husbands or lovers for money or some other material gain in the course of her criminal career. Females make up less than 20 per cent of all serial killers and, unlike male serial killers, are unlikely to have a sexual **motive** but rather kill in order to improve their lifestyle. Many also kill other family members or those close to them, again to profit, and some are also caregivers who kill or harm the people in their care. Infamous examples include Velma Barfield, who killed her fiancé, mother and two elderly people in her care, and Linda Calvey who killed her lover, Ronnie Cook, and whose other lovers all ended up either dead or in prison.

blag

To obtain something by charm, deception or clever talk. Also a violent **robbery** or raid (UK police and general slang); to rob or steal (UK contemporary prison slang).

blank cartridge

Gun **cartridge** that is **loaded** without a **projectile**, so it only causes a sound and/or flash effect.

blank-firing weapon

Object or device that may or may not have the appearance of a **firearm**, originally designed and intended to produce only a sound or flash effect and whose characteristics exclude the firing of any **projectile**, e.g. alarm firearm, starter **pistol/revolver**.

bleater
Sheep-stealer (UK thieves' **cant**, historical slang).

blister agent
Chemical agent that injures the eyes and lungs, burning or blistering the skin. Also known as a vesicant agent.

block
Punishment block (UK contemporary prison slang).

blood agent
Chemical compound that includes the **cyanide** group and affects bodily functions by preventing the normal utilisation of oxygen by body tissues.

bloodborne pathogen
Pathogenic organisms that can cause disease and are present in human blood. These include the human immunodeficiency virus (HIV), hepatitis B (HBV) and hepatitis C (HBC).

bloodstain
Deposit of blood on a surface. ▶ **bloodstain pattern** A grouping or distribution of bloodstains that indicates, through a regular or repetitive form, order or arrangement, the way in which the pattern was deposited or created. ▶ **bloodstain pattern analysis** Bloodstains at a **crime scene** can help **forensic**

investigators deduce what happened and when from the shapes and patterns formed. As blood has to follow the laws of physics, these shapes and patterns are reliable although their analysis is inevitably subjective. A skilled and experienced investigator can yield vital information from bloodstain patterns including the precise nature of events and in what order they occurred as well as whether the crime scene has suffered any disturbance. The analysis can also help pinpoint the positions of victim(s) and perpetrator(s) as well as any witnesses. Bloodstain patterns depend on the speed and distance at which the blood travelled, its volume, the surface it hit and the angle at which it landed, among other factors. Bloodstain pattern analysis can help to corroborate or refute other **evidence**. Bloodstains are either impact stains, passive stains or transfer stains. Blood spatter falls into different categories: **impact spatter** occurs when a force acts upon the blood and causes it to travel through the air before landing on a surface; **projection bloodstains** occur from arterial projection; a spatter of **cast-off bloodstains** occurs when a centrifugal force causes blood to fall or be cast off from a moving, bloodied object; and **expiration bloodstains** are formed from blood exhaled from the mouth.

blood typing

A serologist takes blood samples if relevant at a **crime scene** and then tests them to identify blood type using the ABO system. This system measures antigens and antibodies in the blood.

blow

To expose a **covert agent**, officer, activity or operation, often unintentionally. To have your **cover** blown means to suffer such exposure. Also to inform or reveal information regarding a criminal or crime (UK thieves' **cant**, historical slang).

blow the gab

To confess or inform on an **accomplice** (UK thieves' **cant**, historical slang).

blower

Informer; also a vulgar term for a girl (UK thieves' **cant**, historical slang).

bludger

Violent criminal, taken from 'bludgeon', which was commonly used as a weapon (UK Victorian slang).

bluebottle

Policeman (UK Victorian slang).

blue-light run

See **blues and twos**.

blue-pigeon flyer

Thief who steals the lead or copper from the roofs of churches and houses (UK thieves' **cant**, historical slang).

blues and twos

Urgent and therefore usually fast emergency vehicle journeys. The term derives from the blue flashing lights and originally two-tone siren on police cars and other emergency vehicles. A journey requiring the use of blues and twos is known as a blue-light run (UK police and general slang).

boarding school

Prison or house of correction (UK thieves' **cant**, historical slang).

boated

Transported or **sentenced** to **transportation**. To 'get the boat' is also to receive a particularly harsh sentence (UK historical slang).

bobby

Policeman, derived from Sir Robert Peel, founder of the **Metropolitan Police** (UK Victorian and contemporary slang).

body

Suspect who has been **arrested** and is in **custody** (UK police slang). Also a corpse or dead human being.

body farm

A body farm, or human taphonomy facility (HTF), is a **forensic** research facility that studies the decomposition of the human body. It does so by placing donated human bodies in a variety of situations to decompose naturally, including underwater, buried in various types of soil and hanging from trees. Bodies are also placed in situations that replicate **crime scenes** including being left partially clothed, wrapped in plastic, and placed in a car trunk or in a garbage bin.

B

There are seven body farms in the US, with the first established in 1981 at the University of Tennessee, Knoxville, by the anthropologist Dr William M. Bass. The **Federal Bureau of Investigation** Laboratory's Recovery of Human Remains course is held at the Knoxville facility every year. Body farms are useful to forensic science, especially **forensic anthropology**, and the solving of crimes because they provide information and **evidence** that can help pinpoint the time and nature of a crime. Research at one body farm in the US helped to identify some of the victims of the serial killer **John Wayne Gacy**.

Body farms obtain bodies through donation, either from the family of someone who has died or the person themselves if they have stipulated they want their remains to be used in this manner. A **medical examiner** may also decide to donate an unclaimed and unidentified body to a body farm in the interests of science. All the body farms in the US are part of a university and, as they are located around the country, offer different ecological, climatic and geographical environments for the study of decomposition in varying conditions.

There is also a body farm in the Netherlands and one in Australia, the Australian Facility for Taphonomic Experimental Research (AFTER), which was established because US research on decomposition is often not relevant to the results produced by the Australian environment. Plans to open a body farm in the UK are currently being explored although at present body farms or HFTs are illegal.

body snatcher

Bailiff or police officer (UK thieves' **cant**, historical slang). Also, in the eighteenth and nineteenth centuries, thief who stole bodies from morgues and cemeteries to sell to medical schools and students.

body-worn video (BWV)

Body-worn videos (BWV), sometimes referred to as body-worn cameras, are small, visible devices that are attached to a police officer's uniform, usually on the chest. They are used to capture both video and audio **evidence** when officers are attending incidents. The position of the camera records what happens from the police officer's perspective, acting as an independent witness. Footage is recorded onto an internal, secure storage device and is uploaded at the end of the officer's shift to secure storage for use as evidence at court or other legal proceedings. If it is not required for police purposes it is automatically deleted. BWVs are popular with police forces both in the UK and US as they help build trust in areas where police and community relations are strained, providing evidence in the event of any **allegation** of police brutality or use of unreasonable force and enforcing transparency and accountability.

bolt action

Action of a gun that includes a moveable part that ensures the closing and the locking of a manual repeating **firearm**.

bomb squad

Prisoners sent to clean up an area of a prison into which excrement has been thrown from windows (UK contemporary prison slang). Also a crack-selling crew (US/Jamaican contemporary gang slang).

bona fide

Document or other resource used by the **intelligence** services that backs up or proves an **agent** or officer's claimed identity, often supporting a **cover** story.

BONGO

'Books On, Never Goes Out': an ineffective, lazy or useless police officer also known as a clothes hanger or uniform carrier (UK police slang).

Bonin, William

Bonin (1947–96), aka the Freeway Killer, was an American serial killer, rapist, **hebephile** and ephebophile. The product of a neglected, abusive childhood where he was often left in the care of his convicted child molester grandfather and placed in an orphanage, Bonin started to molest children, including his younger brother, as a teenager. He went on to serve in the Vietnam War where he earned a medal for bravery but also assaulted two soldiers at gunpoint, although this went unreported.

After returning to the US, he began to abduct and **rape** teenage boys, some of whom were hitchhikers, at times acting alone and on other occasions with an **accomplice** named Vernon Butts. His victims were often sodomised, brutally beaten, tortured and then strangled. Bonin also acted with three other accomplices, including William Ray Pugh, a boy he attempted to abduct and rape but who then aided and abetted Bonin in another killing for which he was convicted of manslaughter. Those accomplices testified against

Bonin at his trial and he was given the death penalty. In total, Bonin killed at least twenty-one boys and young men, and is suspected of killing fifteen others.

He was married once, largely to please his mother who hoped it would cure his evident homosexuality, and dated at least one other young woman. He spent fourteen years on death row where he got to know another 'Freeway Killer', Randy Kraft. There is a third, unrelated 'Freeway Killer' named Patrick Kearney. Bonin was executed by **lethal** injection at San Quentin Prison on 23 February 1996, the first person to be executed in this way in the state of California after the gas chamber was declared to be a 'cruel and unusual method' by the state.

bonnet
Undercover assistant to a sharp or card sharp (UK Victorian slang).

boob
Prison (UK contemporary prison slang).

book
Gambling racket based on sporting events. A bookmaker runs 'the book', taking illegal bets.

booking
Police process by which a suspect is officially **arrested** and **charged** with a crime.

books
Membership records of **Mafia** families in the US.

bora, borer

Knife (London contemporary gang slang associated with drill music).

borgata

Italian term meaning neighbourhood or village adopted by the US **Mafia** to mean *famiglia* or family, the established structure and hierarchy of the organisation.

boss

Prison officer (UK contemporary prison slang); gang or **Mafia** leader (contemporary slang).

Boston Strangler

The Boston Strangler is the name given to the person or persons who brutally **assaulted** and murdered at least eleven and possibly thirteen women in and around Boston, Massachusetts, between 1962 and 1964, strangling them with items of their clothing. A local criminal, Albert DeSalvo, confessed to the murders and two more while under **arrest** for the 'Green Man' **rapes** but later recanted his confession. There was no physical **evidence** to link him to the murders and he was stabbed to death in prison in 1973. In 2013, **DNA** from the scene of one of the Boston Strangler's victims, Mary Sullivan, was matched to DNA secretly obtained by police from a water bottle used by DeSalvo's nephew, Timothy. Albert DeSalvo's body was exhumed and the DNA match confirmed but it is still unclear which crimes he committed as some people believe there was more than one Boston Strangler. There have been several movies based on the Boston Strangler murders.

bot

A bot or robot is an automated program that performs designated tasks. Some bots run automatically while others only respond to inputted commands. Some bots are used for malicious purposes and in the perpetration of **cybercrime**. These include denial-of-service (DoS) bots, which bombard websites and applications with multiple access requests in an attempt to override the site or application's security gateway, and spambots, which capture email addresses and add them to **spam** email lists. ▶ **botnet** A botnet is a group of linked computers that have been infected with malicious software and then act together to carry out DoS attacks to try to gain access to other computers and systems.

boundary, barrier

Designated perimeter or area that surrounds a **crime scene** or items of physical **evidence** found at a crime scene. Also known as the perimeter or barrier. Ideally a crime scene has three boundaries or barriers comprising of an outer or public barrier, an inner one for personnel working on the crime scene and a core barrier for the crime scene itself. The first step to securing an outdoor crime scene is to set up the public or outer barrier to prevent **contamination** by the public. This is sometimes called the perimeter containment barrier and is typically when a street, park or open area is cordoned off with **police tape** or vehicles positioned to stop the public from entering.

box

Prison (London contemporary gang slang associated with drill music). Also a **cell** within a cell, also known as a cage (UK contemporary prison slang).

box   47

brain fingerprinting

Also known as Farwell brain fingerprinting, this is a controversial technique that uses electroencephalography (EEG) to record the electrical activity of the brain and find out whether specific information is stored within it. A subject is asked specific questions about a crime with the aim of obtaining a P300 response, a particular kind of brain wave, during a **Concealed Information Test** in which a number of questions are asked about the crime but only one relates to what really happened. It is used as a lie-detection method, but it has raised concerns in the wider scientific community.

breakdown

Shotgun (US contemporary gang slang).

brevity code

Code used to shorten a message but not conceal its content.

brew

Any hot beverage, not just tea; also **alcohol** (UK prison slang).

brick agent

Term used by the **intelligence** services for a field or street **agent**.

brief

Solicitor or **barrister** (UK police, criminal and general slang). Also a police warrant card (UK police slang).

broad arrow

Markings on a prison uniform; 'wearing broad arrow' means serving a prison term (UK Victorian slang).

broading

Cheating at cards with the intention to **swindle**. ▶**broad-sman** Someone who cheats at cards to swindle (UK Victorian slang).

bruckshot

Sawn-off shotgun (London contemporary gang slang associated with drill music).

brush contact

Covert brief encounter between **intelligence** operatives, often prearranged, during which information or material is passed either physically or orally. Also known as a brush pass or a brief encounter.

brute-force attack

A brute-force attack is an attempt to gain access to a computer or system by using multiple successive login attempts with different password and username combinations. The attack can be carried out manually or by using an automated script. **Hackers** often run several systems at the same time similar to a DoS attack (see **bot**) to try to gain access as they may eventually hit upon the right combination, especially if the username or password is short or common. Brute-force attacks are the most common way of compromising online accounts.

BTK

See **Rader, Dennis**.

bubble

To defraud (UK thieves' **cant**, historical slang).

bubird

Pronounced boo-bird. An official **Federal Bureau of Investigation** aeroplane or helicopter.

bucar

Pronounced boo-car. An official **Federal Bureau of Investigation** car.

buccal swab

Buccal means 'relating to the cheek or mouth'. A buccal swab, also known as buccal smear, is a way to collect **DNA** from the cells on the inside of a person's cheek. Buccal swabs are a relatively non-invasive way to collect DNA samples for testing. Their use is very common in police **investigations** where they can include or exclude individuals as suspects.

buck

To shoot someone in the head (US/Jamaican contemporary gang slang).

bucket and pail

Jail (UK cockney rhyming and Victorian slang).

buckshot

Shot with a diameter of greater than 6.1 mm in the English system. In the international metric system, buckshot starts at 5 mm.

bug

Concealed listening device, microphone or other equipment used in audio **surveillance**. ▶**bugged** Room or item that contains a concealed listening device.

bug hunting

Stealing from or cheating drunks, especially at night (UK Victorian slang).

bulk

Someone who serves a **pickpocket** by collecting money from them to store safely elsewhere (UK thieves' **cant**, historical slang).

bulldog with six teeth

Gun (UK Victorian slang).

bullet

Unique **projectile**, most often fired from a gun, which can be spherical or non-spherical and made from a variety of materials. Bullets are shaped or composed differently for a variety of purposes:

- Round-nose – the most commonly found multipurpose **lead bullet**. The end of the bullet is blunted.
- **Hollow-point** – used for controlled penetration. There is a hole in the bullet that expands when it hits its target, creating more damage.
- Jacketed – the soft lead is surrounded by another metal, usually copper, that allows the bullet to penetrate a target more easily (see **full metal jacket**, **total metal jacket**).

- Wadcutter – a bullet specially designed for firing at paper targets. The front of the bullet is flattened.
- Semi-wadcutter – intermediate between round nose and wadcutter.

▶**bullet diameter** The maximum dimension measured across the largest cylindrical section of a bullet.

▶**bullet jacket** The metallic, polymer or plastic envelope surrounding the core of a compound bullet.

▶**bullet trajectory** The curved path of a projectile or bullet from the **muzzle** of a **firearm** to the target. This is more or less straight over short distances close to the muzzle. ▶**bullet wipe** The discoloured area on the immediate periphery of a bullet hole, caused by the transfer of residues from the bearing surface of the bullet. These are dark grey to black residues that typically contain carbon, lead, bullet material and possibly other constituents such as bullet lubricant and **primer** residues. Bullet wipe may occur at any range of fire. Also known as burnishing or leaded edge.

bum beef

False **accusation** or **charge**, or wrongful conviction (US contemporary slang).

bummed

Arrested (UK thieves' **cant**, historical slang).

bum steer

False information or misdirection (US historical slang).

Bundy, Ted

Ted Bundy (1946–89) was one of America's most notorious serial killers who **kidnapped**, **raped** and murdered young women and girls during the 1970s. The exact number of his victims remains unknown, although, before he was executed, he confessed to thirty homicides he had committed between 1974 and 1978. A former law student, Bundy was good looking and charismatic, using both attributes to help him win the trust of his victims.

He would often pretend to be injured or to have a disability and would approach his victims in a public place, asking them to help him put something in his car, the notorious brown Volkswagen Beetle he drove. He would then bludgeon them unconscious before driving them to a secluded spot where he would rape and kill them. He would sometimes revisit the corpses of his victims to groom and perform sexual acts on them until decomposition and destruction by wild animals made this impossible.

He also decapitated at least twelve of his victims and kept some of the severed heads in his apartment, where he slept beside them. Bundy escaped from **custody** on several occasions but, after his final recapture in 1978 in Florida, he received three death **sentences** in two separate trials. Bundy was executed in the electric chair at Florida State prison in 1989. Those who encountered and worked with him described him as a sadistic sociopath and the definition of evil. Bundy described himself as 'the most cold-hearted son of a bitch you'll ever meet'. In 2011 Bundy's complete **DNA** profile was added to the **Federal Bureau of Investigation**'s DNA database in the hope that it might aid the **investigation** of unsolved murder **cases**.

burglary

Burglary is the **theft**, or **attempted** theft, of money or objects from premises where access has not been or is not authorised. Damage to premises that appears to have been caused by a person attempting to enter to commit a burglary is also counted as burglary. Residential and commercial burglaries are distinguished by the function of the building.

burn

Tobacco or cigarettes (UK contemporary prison slang).

burned

When an **intelligence agent** or officer is **compromised**, they are said to be burned. This can also be used to describe when the target of a **surveillance** operation realises that they are being watched or followed.

burner

Handgun (London contemporary gang slang associated with drill). Also a temporary, disposable mobile phone bought with prepaid minutes and paid for in cash so it cannot be easily traced (UK/US contemporary slang).

Bureau

Federal Bureau of Investigation agents generally refer to the organisation as 'The Bureau', especially when speaking to other agents.

burst

To shoot (London contemporary gang slang associated with drill music).

burst-fire weapon

Type of **automatic firearm** that fires a predetermined number of shots with each pull of the **trigger**.

buster

Burglar (UK Victorian slang).

butt

In **handguns** it is the bottom part of the **grip**. In longer guns such as **rifles**, it is the rear or shoulder end of the **stock**.

buttock and file

Pickpocket (UK thieves' **cant**, historical slang).

buttoner

Sharper or card sharp's assistant who entices people to play (UK Victorian slang).

buzzing

Stealing. Most commonly used to describe **pickpocketing** (UK Victorian slang).

BWV

See **body-worn video**.

C

cache

Hidden stock of supplies that typically contains items such as food, water, medical items, and/or communications equipment, which is packaged to prevent damage from exposure. A cache can be buried, submerged or concealed in some other way and is usually designed to support an **agent**, officer or operative who is isolated and operating alone.

CAD

See **Computer-Aided Dispatch**.

CAIT

See **Child Abuse Investigation Team**.

calibre

A measurement of **barrel** diameter, but commonly used to identify, in association with other elements such as the length of the **cartridge case** or brand, the type of cartridge a gun is designed to fire.

call sign

Any combination of characters or pronounceable words that is used to establish and maintain communications, and which identifies a communication facility, a command, an authority, an activity or a unit.

Camargo Barbosa, Daniel

Camargo Barbosa (1930–94) was a Colombian serial killer who **raped** and murdered up to 150 young girls in the 1970s and 1980s, making him one of the most prolific serial killers of all time. He chose poor, vulnerable young girls because he was obsessed with virgins and the pain he inflicted upon them gave him greater satisfaction. Camargo Barbosa was stabbed to death in prison at the age of sixty-four by a fellow prisoner who turned out to be the nephew of one of his victims.

Camp Peary

Camp Peary is a 9,000-acre training facility in Virginia, USA, which hosts a **covert Central Intelligence Agency** training facility known as 'The Farm'. It is also known as Camp Swampy. Although it is well known that this facility exists, it has never been formally acknowledged by the US government.

can

Prison (UK contemporary slang).

canary bird

Prison inmate (UK thieves' **cant**, historical slang). To 'do **bird**' is still used as contemporary slang to mean to serve time in prison.

cannabis, marijuana

The most used illegal recreational **drug** in the world, cannabis or marijuana is a psychoactive drug from the cannabis plant that is also used for medical purposes. It is usually smoked or eaten. Various names given to cannabis refer to the different methods of preparation. Weed refers to the dried buds and leaves of the plant while hashish or hash is prepared from cannabis resin. Weed and hashish are commonly smoked in hand-rolled cigarettes known as joints but can also be smoked in pipes or bongs. Cannabis is also cooked into food, especially cookies and brownies, before being eaten. Cannabis is an important part of the illegal global **drug-trafficking** trade and is the drug seized in the greatest quantities worldwide. Also known as: 420; A-bomb (cannabis mixed with **heroin**); Acapulco gold; Acapulco red; ace; African black; African bush; airplane; alfalfa; *alfombra*; Alice B. Toklas; all-star; *almohada*; Angola; animal cookie (hydroponic); Arizona; ash; Aunt Mary; AZ; baby; bale; *bambalachacha*; Barbara Jean; *bareta*; bash; bazooka (cannabis mixed with **cocaine** paste); B. C. Budd; Bernie; bhang; big pillow; biggy; bionic (cannabis mixed with **PCP**); black bart; black gold; black Maria; blondie; blue cheese; blue crush; blue dream; blue jeans; blue sage; blueberry; bobo bush; boo; boom; branches; broccoli; bud; budda; *burrito verde*; bush; cabbage; café; *cajita*; cali; camara; Canadian black; catnip; *cheeba*; Chernobyl; cheese; Chicago black; Chicago green; chippie; *chistosa*; Christmas tree; chronic; churro; cigar; citrol; cola; Colorado cocktail; cookie (hydroponic); *cotorrito*; crazy weed; creeper bud; crippy; crying weed; *culican*; dank; devil's lettuce; dew; diesel; dimba; dinkie dow; *diosa verde*; dirt grass; ditch weed; dizz; *djamba*; dody; dojo; domestic; *Donna Juana*; doobie; downtown brown; drag weed; dro (hydroponic); *droski* (hydroponic); dry high; *elefante pata*; endo; *escoba*; fattie; fine stuff; fire; flower; flower tops; fluffy; fuzzy lady; *gallina*; *gallito*; garden; *garifa*; gauge; gangster; ganja; gash; gato; Ghana; gigi (hydroponic); giggle smoke; giggle weed; girl scout cookie (hydroponic); Gloria; gold; gold leaf; gold star; gong; good giggles; gorilla; gorilla glue;

granddaddy purp; grass; grasshopper; green; green crack; green-eyed girl; green eye; green goblin; green goddess; green Mercedes Benz; green paint; green skunk; greenhouse; *grenuda*; *greta*; *guardada*; gummy bears; *gunga*; hairy one; hash; Hawaiian; hay; hemp; herb; *hierba*; holy grail; homegrown; hooch; *hoja*; *humo*; hydro; Indian boy; Indian hay; Jamaican gold; Jamaican red; jane; jive; jolly green; jon-jem; joy smoke; *Juan Valdez*; *juanita*; jungle juice; kaff; kali; kaya; KB; Kentucky blue; KGB; khalifa; kiff; killa; kilter; King Louie; kona gold; kumba; kush; laughing grass; laughing weed; leaf; *lechuga*; lemon-lime; *leña*; *liamba*; lime pillows; little green friends; little smoke; *llesca*; loaf; lobo; loco weed; loud; love nuggets; love weed; Lucas; MJ; machinery; *macoña*; *mafafa*; magic smoke; Manhattan silver; *manteca*; *maracachafa*; Maria; marimba; *mariquit*a; Mary Ann; Mary Jane; Mary Jones; Mary Warner; Mary Weaver; matchbox; *matraca*; Maui wowie; Meg; method; mersh; Mexican brown; Mexicali haze; Mexican green; Mexican red; MMJ; mochie (hydroponic); *moña*; monte; moocah; mootie; mora; *morisqueta*; *mostaza*; mota; mother; mowing the lawn; muggie; my brother; narizona; northern lights; nug; O-boy; OG; OJ; owl; paja; palm; Paloma; *Palomita*; Panama cut; Panama gold; Panama red; *pakalolo*; parsley; *pasto*; pasture; *peliroja*; *pelosa*; phoenix; pine; Pink Panther; pintura; plant; platinum cookie (hydroponic); platinum Jack; pocket rocket; popcorn; *porro*; pot; pretendo; Prop 215; puff; purple haze; purple OG; Queen Ann's lace; red hair; ragweed; railroad weed; rainy day woman; Rasta weed; red cross; red dirt; reefer; reggie; *repollo*; righteous bush; root; rope; Rosa Maria; salt and pepper; Santa Marta; sassafras; sativa; shoe; sinsemilla; shmagma; shora; shrimp; shwag; skunk; Skywalker (hydroponic); smoke; smoochy woochy poochy; smoke Canada;

sour OG; spliff; stems; sticky; stink weed; sugar weed; sweet Lucy; Tahoe (hydroponic); tangy OG; terp; terpene; Tex-Mex; Texas tea; tigitty; *tila*; tims; top shelf; Tosca; train wreck; tree; trinity OG; tweed; *valle*; wake and bake; weed; weed tea; wet (cannabis dipped in **PCP**); wheat; white-haired lady; wooz; Yellow Submarine; yen pop; yerba; *yesca*; young girls; *zacate*; *zacatecas*; *zambi*; zip; zoom (cannabis mixed with PCP).

cant, thieves' cant

Cant is a jargon belonging to and used by a particular group or sub-group. From the sixteenth to nineteenth centuries in England, thieves and other marginal members of society had their own cant, known as thieves' cant, which they used to communicate without being rumbled by the authorities. The Artful Dodger in Dickens's *Oliver Twist* speaks almost entirely in cant, and Dickens helpfully included a thieves' cant glossary at the back of the book. Thieves' cant was also known as 'flash' or 'peddler's French' and existed across Europe in different forms.

It began to flourish in sixteenth-century England when there was less work available and, as a result, crime started to rise. The new burgeoning underclass of thieves and rogues met in public gathering places or 'flash houses' in order to share tips and information. Much as people have an interest in true crime today to arm themselves with knowledge, so the general population became fascinated with this underclass and several thieves' cant dictionaries were published as a result.

These dictionaries contained not just definitions of the words or jargon used by thieves and vagabonds but also descriptions of their various scams so the public could be forewarned. An early example was John Awdeley's *The Fraternity of Vagabonds*, where Awdeley explains that he gathered the information for his book by interviewing 'ruffling and beggarly' people who insisted on remaining anonymous for fear of being killed in retribution by their brethren.

Thieves' cant dictionaries were so popular they were published in other countries, including the US where, in 1859, a New York police chief named George W. Matsell published *The Rogue's Lexicon*. There was also a French–English cant dictionary. The origins of thieves' cant remain a mystery, but it is generally believed to be a mixture of English, Romany, French, Yiddish, Latin and Italian influences with some words from other European languages including German and Portuguese. Thieves' cant fell out of use after the nineteenth century but remnants of it may be found in children's songs, cockney rhyming slang and Polari, a form of nineteenth-century cant used by the gay subculture, actors, showmen, the British Merchant Navy and wrestlers as well as thieves and prostitutes. The game Dungeons and Dragons keeps the tradition alive with its own fictional criminal cant.

C

capo

Used to mean the **boss** in **Mafia** terms but now refers to a captain or lieutenant within a Mafia family. ▶ *capo dei capi* The ultimate leader or crime boss in a Sicilian or American Mafia family.

car

Group of prisoners who stick, or 'ride', together in the prison yard and back each other up if necessary. Cars are organised by race, religion, gang or other affiliation. ▶ **in the car** In on a deal or taking part in a plan involving other inmates while in prison (US contemporary prison slang).

carbine

Rifle of relatively short length and light weight originally designed for mounted troops.

carbon

Paper that is impregnated with chemicals that can reveal **secret writing**. This is often concealed within a writing pad to appear like a normal sheet of paper.

carpet

Three-year **sentence** (UK contemporary prison slang).

car toss

Type of **dead drop** in which the documents or information are concealed and thrown into a preselected location from a car travelling along a designated route. Concealment devices might, for example, be drink cans or bottles, and could include a tracking device so that the intended **agent** could find the item. (See **toss**.)

cartridge

Unit of **ammunition** made up of a cartridge case, **primer**, powder and **bullet**. Also called a **round** or **load**. A gun cartridge consists of a self-contained unit comprising the primer, **propellant** and one or more **projectiles**, unless it is a **blank cartridge**, all housed within a cartridge case.

▶ **cartridge case** Component of a gun cartridge that contains the primer and propellant. ▶ **cartridge case mouth** Open end of a cartridge case or **shotgun** cartridge from which the projectile or **shot charge** is expelled in firing. ▶ **cartridge head** End of the gun cartridge case in which the primer or priming is inserted and the surface upon which the headstamp identification is imprinted. The head impacts against the breech during firing. ▶ **cartridge headstamp** Numerals, letters and symbols or a combination of these stamped into the head of a cartridge case or shotgun cartridge to identify the manufacturer, year of manufacture, **calibre** or **gauge**, and other additional information.

CARVER

Special forces acronym that stands for 'Criticality, Accessibility, Recuperability, Vulnerability, Effect and Recognizability'.

carving

Forensic carving, also known as data carving, is the process of extracting a collection of data from a larger data set in **digital forensics**. Data carving frequently occurs during a digital **investigation** when the unallocated file system spaces are analysed in order to extract files. The files are 'carved' from the unallocated space.

case

The **investigation** of a crime from the time it is reported/discovered until it is resolved or closed. Also a brothel (UK thieves' **cant**, historical slang). Contemporary sex workers still refer to 'going case', meaning to leave a club or other premises where they are working as a hostess or dancer in

order to perform sexual acts for money. ▶**case file**
Collection of documents relating to a particular case or
investigation. These can be kept in files, folders, boxes, cabi-
nets and drawers, and can include photographs, video and
audio recordings as well as laboratory reports, media clip-
pings and recordings, and documented **evidence**. ▶**case
identifier** Unique combination of letters, numbers and
sometimes symbols used to identify a particular case.
▶**caseload** Number of cases that an investigator is
actively investigating. ▶**case officer** In the **intelligence**
services, case officers manage **agent** networks, principal
agents, agents and **assets**. They also spot potential agents
and recruit them as well as training them in **tradecraft**.
▶**case review** Comprehensive review of all case-related
documents and evidence for the purpose of solving the case.
▶**case summary** Documentation summarising the status
of a **cold case** after review.

cast

Technique to preserve and replicate impression **evidence**
in soft material such as soil, tissue or snow. Casts can be
made of shoeprints, bitemarks, tyre prints and toolmarks.
When done properly, casting produces excellent positive
replicas of the impression, but casts are not exact
duplicates.

cast-off bloodstain

Cast-off **bloodstains**, as their name suggests, occur when
centrifugal force causes blood to fall or be cast off from a
moving, bloodied object such as a weapon which has been
flung through the air. Cessation cast-off patterns occur
when that object suddenly stops moving, e.g. when the
weapon lands on the floor after it has been flung. These

bloodstains are particularly difficult to interpret as there are so many possible variations of movement, speed, angle and whether or not the blood has been repeatedly thrown. There are, however, characteristic patterns that occur and which can offer some clue as to what took place at the **crime scene**.

cat
Drunk, fighting prostitute (UK thieves' **cant**, historical slang). Also a convict or prisoner (UK contemporary prison slang).

catfish
Fake or stolen online identity used, especially on social media, to deceive, abuse or troll people. Catfishing is frequently used for romance or relationship scams on dating sites and/or to defraud unsuspecting victims. Sexual predators including **paedophiles**, **cyber-bullies** and trolls are all known to catfish, and it is also used in **espionage** to blackmail or discredit the target. Catfishing can result in serious **sexual assaults** including **rape**, the loss of money and reputation, and even suicide as a result of the impact on the victim. Although catfishing in itself is not, in most instances, a **cybercrime**, it is often used to facilitate it.

CC
'Cop on the corner' or in the area (US contemporary gang slang).

CCO
See **civilian communications officer**.

CCTV

See **closed-circuit television**.

CCW

See **concealed carry**.

cell

Usually small room in a prison, police station or other institution to which someone is confined. Also, a subordinate organisation formed around a specific process, capability or activity within a designated larger organisation, and which is often used in relation to terrorists.

cement shoes

Popular murder method to get rid of someone who has fallen out of favour with an **organised crime** gang or the **Mafia** where someone is weighted down, dead or alive, before being thrown in water in the hope that they will sink and never be found.

Central Intelligence Agency (CIA)

The Central Intelligence Agency is an independent US government **agency** responsible for collecting, evaluating, analysing and disseminating national and foreign security **intelligence** to assist the President and senior officials in making decisions affecting national security. It officially comprises the Directorate of Intelligence, the Directorate of Science and Technology, the Directorate of Support and the NCS (National Clandestine Service). The Special Activities Division (SAD) is the NCS's **covert** and **clandestine** operations unit.

CEOP Command

See **Child Exploitation and Online Protection Command**.

chaff

Reflector that consists of thin, narrow metallic strips of various lengths and frequency responses, which is used to reflect radar echoes to create confusion.

chain of custody

Also known as the chain of **evidence**. The chronological paper trail that documents who collected, handled, analysed or otherwise controlled a piece of evidence during an **investigation**. It is vital that a proper chain of custody is established and adhered to without gaps or discrepancies to rule out the possibility of mishandling or tampering with the evidence. Evidence can be ruled inadmissible and therefore suppressed where the chain of custody has not been properly secured and there is therefore no way of being able to trust the accuracy of, for example, **fingerprint** analysis or blood tests.

chamber

Essential part of a **firearm** into which the **cartridge** is inserted prior to being fired. In a **revolver**, the chamber is not part of the **barrel** but is instead made by holes in the **cylinder** that have been formed to accept a cartridge.

change detection

Image-enhancement technique that compares two images of the same area from different time periods, eliminating identical picture elements in order to leave the parts that have changed.

charge

Formal **accusation** against a person that a criminal offence has been committed.

Also, in relation to a gun **cartridge**, the amount, by weight, of a component of that cartridge (i.e. priming weight, **propellant** weight, **shot** weight).

charm

Lockpick (UK thieves' **cant**, historical slang).

cheap thief

Someone who steals from churches (US historical slang).

chef (up)

To stab or kill (London contemporary gang slang associated with drill music).

chemical agent

Chemical substance used with the intention to kill, seriously injure or incapacitate through its physiological effects.

chemical enhancement

Use of chemicals that react with particular types of **evidence** such as blood, **latent fingerprints** and semen that might otherwise be difficult to detect. These chemicals include fluorescein and **luminol** for blood, and iodine, silver nitrate, ninhydrin and cyanoacrylate (or superglue) for fingerprints.

chemical hazard

Any **toxic** chemical manufactured, used, transported or stored that can cause death or other harm. This includes

chemical agents and **chemical weapons** prohibited under the Chemical Weapons Convention as well as toxic industrial chemicals.

chemical weapon

Under the Chemical Weapons Convention, the definition of a chemical weapon includes all **toxic** chemicals and their precursors, except when used for purposes permitted by the Convention. Any munitions or devices specifically designed to inflict harm or cause death through the release of toxic chemicals are chemical weapons, including but not limited to mortars, artillery shells, missiles, bombs, mines or spray tanks. This includes any equipment specifically designed for use 'directly in connection' with the employment of the munitions and devices identified as chemical weapons.

chief constable

Chief constable is the rank used by every chief police officer of the territorial and special national British police forces except the **Metropolitan Police Service** and **City of London Police**, where the head is the commissioner. (The formal title of the Met's chief officer is the 'Commissioner of Police of the Metropolis'.) The rank is also used by the chief officers of the three principal Crown Dependency police forces, the States of Guernsey and Jersey Police Services and the Isle of Man Constabulary, as well as by some chief police officers in Canada. A chief constable is appointed by the police and crime commissioner of their service and has no senior officer.

chief inspector

Rank of UK police officer above that of inspector and below that of **superintendent**. They oversee response teams, police neighbourhood teams, the **Criminal Investigation Department**, **investigations** and/or offender management. They also act as senior public order or **firearms** commanders and critical incident managers.

chief superintendent

Rank of UK police officer above that of **superintendent** and below that of **assistant chief constable** (or **commander** in the **Metropolitan Police**). They are responsible to the chief constable for all policing activity in their area. All local partnership, crime and operations matters are directed to them in their capacity as police chief.

Chikatilo, Andrei

Andrei Romanovich Chikatilo (1936–94) was a Soviet citizen who was one of the most prolific serial killers of all time, operating between 1978 and 1990. Chikatilo sexually **assaulted** and mutilated his victims, all of whom were women and children, including boys. He was known as the Butcher of Rostov, the Red Ripper and the Rostov Ripper, Rostov being the region of Russia where most of the murders took place. He enjoyed tasting his victims' blood as well as consuming body parts that included tongues and nipples. When he was caught in 1990 he confessed to fifty-six murders, was **charged** with fifty-three and **sentenced** to death for fifty-two of them. Chikatilo's **case** is noteworthy not just because of the number and brutality of his crimes but also because he belonged to a rare group of people known as non-secretors whose blood type can only be inferred from a blood sample as it did not match that of his other bodily fluids. Chikatilo's blood was Type A and his semen Type AB. Police only had a sample of semen from the victims when they first caught and **arrested** him in 1984 for a series of minor offences so he escaped a murder charge. He was finally caught thanks in part to psychological **profiling** carried out by a psychiatrist, Alexander Bhukanovsky, who refined an earlier profile. When Bhukanovsky's profile was read out to him, Chikatilo was so flattered he confessed to the murders and even led police to the remains of bodies that had hitherto been undiscovered. Chikatilo was executed with a single shot to the back of his head in 1994 in Moscow Prison. Bhukanovsky went on to become a sought-after expert on sexual crimes and serial killers.

Child Abuse Investigation Team (CAIT)

Team within UK police forces responsible for investigating crimes relating to minors.

Child Exploitation and Online Protection Command

CEOP Command is a division of the UK **National Crime Agency** that works both nationally and internationally to track down and prosecute online child sex offenders, including those involved in the production, distribution and viewing of child abuse material. CEOP Command's units include the **Missing Persons Unit** and the **Missing Children's Team**, which endeavour to trace missing people.

CHIMPS

'Can't Help In Most Police Situations' – a derogatory term applied to **police community support officers** (UK police slang acronym).

ching

A knife or to stab (London contemporary gang slang associated with drill music).

chink-chink

Sound that cups or mugs make when knocked or tapped together. Called over a police radio to alert officers that a **brew**'s up (UK police slang). If there is more than one possible station where the brew might be obtained, this is followed by the **call sign** of the relevant station. Less popular now that many police officers have to rely on high-street outlets rather than catering facilities in police stations.

chirp

Inform (UK Victorian slang).

CHIS

See **covert human intelligence source**.

chloroform

Chloroform is well known for its use in anaesthesia but it is also a deadly **poison**, requiring only 1.5 ounces or around a shot-glass measure to kill. In 2018, three-year-old Mariah Woods from North Carolina died from chloroform **toxicity** and her mother's boyfriend, Earl Kimrey, was **charged** with first-degree murder. In the UK in 2015, two brothers were jailed for the murder of Sameena Imam with chloroform after she had demanded one of them leave his partner for her. Craig McCreight was jailed for life in Scotland in 2002 for the murder of his partner with chloroform but had his conviction quashed in 2009 due to flawed scientific **evidence**. Even when chloroform was used as an anaesthetic, numerous accidental deaths occurred due to its high levels of toxicity, which is why its use is now tightly regulated, although it can be made from combining easily available household substances including bleach and acetone.

chummy

Police nickname for a suspect who is under **arrest**. Instead of referring to the person by their name, the officer will speak of them as 'Chummy' (UK police slang).

chune up

To **assault** or beat up (London contemporary gang slang associated with drill music).

CIA

See **Central Intelligence Agency**.

CID

See **Criminal Investigation Department**.

cipher

A cipher is a way to conceal words or text using encryption. Cipher can also refer to the words or text that have been encrypted, the key used to encrypt or the method of encryption. A cipher pad is a pad of paper sheets that have a non-repetitive key printed on them. A sheet is used once to **encipher** text and another sheet is used once to decipher it.

circumstantial evidence

Circumstantial **evidence** is indirect evidence that is indicative but not conclusive. Much **forensic** evidence is circumstantial because a jury must make a connection between, for example, a **fingerprint** found at a **crime scene** and the actual crime that occurred.

CIT

See **Concealed Information Test**.

City of London Police

Founded in 1839, this is the force responsible for the City of London (primarily the financial district), and is distinct from the much larger **Metropolitan Police Service**, which looks after the rest of the city.

civilian communications officer (CCO)

CCOs are the people who handle 999 or emergency calls, taking all necessary information and giving advice where appropriate. They also constantly monitor radio channels and maintain continuous contact with operational officers so they can provide information from police computers.

clandestine

In **intelligence**, military and police terms, any activity or operation sponsored or conducted by governmental departments or agencies with the intent to assure secrecy and concealment. See also **black**.

clap

Shot, 'He clapped him' (US/Jamaican contemporary gang slang).

claret

Blood (UK thieves' **cant**, historical slang still in contemporary use).

classified

Official designation given to a document or information that is deemed of sufficient importance or interest to require protection against **unauthorised disclosure** in the interests of national security.

clean

Free of any kind of **surveillance** or unknown to hostile **intelligence**. Can refer to an object such as a phone or an environment as well as a person.

clearance rate

Percentage of crimes known to the police or **law enforcement** that were 'cleared', or solved, by **arrest** or other special circumstances. The clearance rate is calculated by dividing the number of known crimes by the number of cleared or solved ones.

clickjack

Exploit that occurs when a cybercriminal tricks someone into clicking on a hyperlink, thinking they are being taken to a particular site or URL when they are, in fact, taken elsewhere, usually for malicious purposes including downloading **malware** or harvesting their personal information.

clip

Cartridge container used to rapidly **reload** the **magazine** of a **firearm**. Also known as a stripper clip.

clive

Knife (UK thieves' **cant**, historical slang).

closed case

Case where all suspects have been identified and, if possible, successfully prosecuted.

closed-circuit television (CCTV)

Closed-circuit television (CCTV) is used for monitoring and surveillance purposes, primarily for security reasons. CCTV consists of unmanned, remotely mounted video cameras that transmit live pictures back to a monitoring system. The signals are not publicly distributed although the signal may travel on wireless networks. CCTV is used in town centres and on roads as well as in airports, hospitals, government buildings and on public transport. It is also used to protect private property and by companies and organisations such as banks, shops, shopping malls and at ATMs or cashpoints. CCTV footage is often used to help identify suspects in a crime and for investigative purposes such as establishing the movements of suspects and their vehicles. Following its inception in the 1970s, the images produced are now of much higher quality and CCTV cameras have proliferated to the extent that concerns have been raised over their misuse. CCTV can also be used for criminal purposes, with tiny cameras attached to ATMs recording PIN numbers as they are entered. In the UK the Data Protection Act 1998 regulates the use of CCTV, as does the subsequent 2012 Protection of Freedoms Act. Similarly, in other countries local and national laws govern its use and that of the obtained data, with Sweden requiring permits for any public operator, including the police, but in the United States, the use of CCTV is not as tightly regulated.

close-up photograph

Close-up photographs are taken to capture specific items of **evidence**. They should provide enough detail for positive identification of the evidence and for **forensic** analysis when appropriate. A ruler is used to show scale when taking close-up photographs, placed on the same plane as the evidence.

cocaine

Cocaine is a highly **addictive** white powder that is commonly snorted but can also be inhaled as **crack cocaine** or freebase or, most dangerously, injected. It triggers a flood of dopamine, which causes a state of euphoria but over time the **drug** alters the way the brain releases dopamine so that frequent users need more and more of it to attain the same state or even to feel normal. It increases the risk of stroke and heart attacks. Prolonged use, if snorted, causes damage to the nose cartilage that separates the nostrils. Cocaine is a Class A drug in the UK, a Schedule II drug in the US and illegal in most other countries except, in some instances, for personal or medical use. Globally, it is the second most popular illegal recreational drug after **cannabis**. Also known as: Adidas; all-American drug; *ancla*; angel powder; Angie; animals; A-1; Apache; *apodo*; *arriba*; Audi; Aunt Nora; *azucar*; baby powder; *barrato*; *basuco*; bazooka (cocaine paste mixed with **cannabis**); beach; Belushi (cocaine mixed with heroin); Bernice; Bernie's flakes; Bernie's gold dust; big bird; big bloke; big C; big flake; big rush; Billie Hoke; bird; birdie powder; *blanca nieves*; *blanco*; blast; blizzard; blonde; blocks; blow; BMW; board; bobo; *bolitas*; Bolivian marching powder; *bombita* (cocaine mixed with heroin); booger sugar; bose; bouncing powder; *brisa*; bump; C-dust; *caballo*; *caca*; Cadillac; California pancakes; calves; *canelon*; candy; car; carney;

carrie nation; cars; case; *cebolla*; Cecil; cement; charlie; chevy; Cheyenne; *chica*; *chicanitas*; *chinos*; *chiva*; *cielo*; clear

kind; clear tires; coca; Coca-Cola; *cocazo*; coconut; coke; cola; Colorado; *comida*; *comida dulce*; Connie; cookie; *cosa*; *coso*; *cosos*; crow; crusty treats; *cuadro*; Death Valley; designer jeans; devil's dandruff; diamonds; diente; dienton; diesel; diosa blanca; dona blanca; double bubble; double letters; dove; dream; *dulces*; Duracell; *durazno*; *duro*; dust; *escama*; *escorpino*; *falopa*; Fef1; *fichas*; fiesta; fire (cocaine base); fish (liquid cocaine); fish scale; flake; flea-market jeans; Florida snow; flour; food; foolish powder; fox; freeze; friskie powder; frula; funtime; *gabacho*; galaxy; *gallos*; *gato*; gift of the sun; gin; girl; girlfriend; glad stuff; gold dust; green gold; *gringa*; *gringito*; grout; *guerillo*; *gueros*; guitar; H1; hai hit; hamburger; happy dust; happy powder; happy trails; heaven; heaven dust; heavy one; hen; Henry VIII; HH; HHJ; high heat; HMH; hooter; *hundai*; hunter; ice cream; icing; Inca message; Izzy; jam; *Jaime blanco*; *jaula*; jeep; jelly; John Deere; joy flakes; joy powder; *juguetes*; jump rope; junk; K13; king's habit; *kordell*; *la familia*; lady; lady snow; late night; *lavada*; leaf; *libreta*; line; loaf; love affair; LV; maca flour; *madera*; Mama Coca; *mandango*; *manita*; Maradona; *marbol*; material; mayback (62 grams); mayo; *melcocha*; *media lata*; Mercedes; milk; *milonga*; mojo; Mona Lisa; *monte*; *morro*; mosquitos; movie-star drug; *muchacha*; *muebles*; *mujer*; napkin; *nieve*; *niña*; nine-two-one; normal; nose candy; nose powder; old lady; oyster stew; paint; Paloma; *paleta*; *palomos*; *pantalones*; papas; paradise; paradise white; parrot; pearl; *pedrito*; *perico*; personal; Peruvian; Peruvian flake; Peruvian lady; *pescado*; *peta*; *pez*; *pichicata*; pillow; pimp; *pingas*; pingos; *pintura blanca*; *poli*; *pollo*; *polvo*; powder; powder diamonds; puma; *puritain*; *quadros*; *queso blanco*; racehorse charlie; Rambo; *refresco*; *refrescas*;

regular kind; regular work; reindeer dust; Richie; rims; rocky mountain; Rolex; Rolex HH; rooster; scale; *schmeck*; schoolboy; scorpion; scottie; seed; Serpico; seven; seven-seven; seven-seven-seven; sierra; six-two; shirt; ski equipment; sleigh ride; sneeze; sniff; snow; snow bird; snow cone; snow white; snowball; snowflake; society high; soda; *soditas*; soft; space (cocaine mixed with **PCP**); special; speedball (cocaine mixed with heroin); stardust; star-spangled powder; studio fuel; suave; sugar; Superman; sweet stuff; *tabique*; *tablas*; *talco*; *talquito*; *tamales*; taxi; *tecate*; teenager; teeth; tequila; thunder; tire; tonto; toot; *tortes*; *tortuga*; Toyota; T-shirts; tubo; *tucibi* (pink variety); turkey; tutti-frutti; *vaquita*; wash; wet; whack (cocaine mixed with PCP); white; white bitch; white cross; white dove; white girl; white goat; white horse; white lady; white Mercedes Benz; white mosquito; white paint; white powder; white rock; white root; white shirt; white T; white wall tires; whitey; whiz bang; wings; woolly; work; *yayo*; *yeyo*; *yoda*; *zapato*; zip.

cock

To place the **hammer**, **firing pin** or striker of a **firearm** in position for firing.

code

System in which arbitrary letters or symbols are substituted for words or text to conceal them. ▶ **code book** Book containing **codes** and the plain text equivalents used by the **intelligence** services and military.

Code 11

Off duty (UK police slang).

Code 4
Meal break (UK police slang).

C

CODIS
See **Combined DNA Index System**.

coercion
Coercion occurs when someone is forced to behave in a particular way, for example by threats of violence. The person concerned does not act freely.

cognitive bias
Tendency to evaluate or perceive information based on the experience and unconscious preferences held rather than on the facts alone. A confirmation bias is a type of cognitive bias and is the tendency to look for or interpret information that confirms a pre-existing belief or hypothesis. Cognitive biases can result in subjectivity and distorted thinking, leading to flawed decision making or interpretation during **investigations** or **forensic** examinations.

cokehead
Cocaine addict (contemporary slang).

coldbath jug
Prison (UK Victorian slang). Possibly from Coldbath Fields prison, built in 1794 and closed in 1877, which was also known as Clerkenwell Gaol. It was located at the junction of Farringdon Road and Rosebery Avenue in Clerkenwell, London, on the site of what is now Mount Pleasant Mail Centre. The prison gates were incorporated into the original post office and demolished in 1901.

cold case

Criminal **investigation** that has not been solved and is not being actively investigated due to lack of **evidence** or **leads**. There is always the possibility that new information could be received or emerge, which may reopen the active investigation. Famous cold **cases** include the Black Dahlia, **Jack the Ripper** and the **Zodiac Killer**. *Cold Case* (2003 to 2010) was also a US TV series based in a fictional Philadelphia police department specialising in cold cases.

▶ **cold-case unit** Dedicated police or **law enforcement** unit that consists of two or more investigators whose specific job it is to investigate cold cases.

cold hit

Connection identified between two criminal **cases** that were not previously known to be related. A **DNA** cold hit is a connection made between a crime-scene DNA profile and a DNA profile found in a DNA database in the absence of any prior investigative **leads**.

cold pitch

An attempt to recruit an **asset**, contact or **agent** without prior development, interaction or contact.

collector

Highwayman or highway robber (UK thieves' **cant**, historical slang).

Combined DNA Index System (CODIS)

This is the **Federal Bureau of Investigation** system that can link **DNA** found at **crime scenes** and so identify serial offenders. There are three levels of CODIS: the Local DNA Index System (LDIS), used by individual laboratories; the

State DNA Index System (SDIS), which serves as a state's DNA database containing DNA profiles from LDIS laboratories; and the National DNA Index System (NDIS), managed by the FBI as the nation's DNA database containing all DNA profiles uploaded by participating states.

comedown

Occurs when the effects of a **drug** begin to wear off and the user experiences symptoms similar to a hangover from **alcohol**. In both instances, the body is trying to process the **toxic** effects of what are essentially **poisons** to the system with the resulting headache or heavy head and need to sleep or lie down.

command and control

Command and control (C & C) is the authority and capability of an organisation to direct the actions of its personnel and the use of its equipment. The principles of command and control can be scaled and used to resolve incidents and operations ranging in size and scope, from the policing of a local community event to a major criminal **investigation** such as a major terrorist attack that involves mobilising several police forces.

commander

The rank of commander is common within naval and air forces and is also used within several other organisations, including London's **Metropolitan Police Service** and **City of London Police** services. It is a chief officer rank, senior to chief superintendent. In the Metropolitan Police Service, it is junior to deputy assistant commissioner and in the City of London Police it is junior to **assistant chief constable**. It is equivalent to the rank of assistant chief constable in other police forces.

commissioner

Title of both the head of the **Metropolitan Police Service** and the head of the **City of London Police**. (See **chief constable**.)

communications intelligence (comint)

Information or **intelligence** that has been found, intercepted or otherwise obtained by agencies or governments other than the intended recipients.

communications network (comnet)

Organisation of stations capable of intercommunication, but not necessarily on the same channel.

communications security (comsec)

Security measures designed to deny unauthorised access to valuable information that might be gained from telecommunications or to mislead unauthorised people in their interpretation of those telecommunications.

Company

Those on the inside of the **Central Intelligence Agency** refer to it as 'The Company'.

comparison sample

Generic term used to describe physical material or **evidence** discovered at **crime scenes** that may be compared with samples from people, tools and physical locations. Comparison samples may be from either an unknown or a known source.

Comparison Question Test (CQT)

Also known as the Probable Lie Test, this is a directly accusatory method of questioning, used alongside a **polygraph test**, which detects deceit in the subject's physiological responses to questions such as 'Did you kill her?'

complaint

Formal written **accusation** made by someone, often a prosecutor, and filed in court or to an official body, alleging that a specific person, or persons, has committed a specific offence.

compromised

When an operation, **agent** or **asset** has been uncovered and is no longer secret or when a piece of **classified** information has been passed to hostile **intelligence** or governments.

Computer-Aided Dispatch (CAD)

Computer-Aided Dispatch is the allocation and dispatch of police and other emergency services, with the aid of computer software, in response to emergency calls. When a crime is reported, a CAD number is allocated to it. Computer-Aided Dispatch is also used in the private sector by, for example, taxi firms.

computer forensics

See **digital forensics**.

con

Convict or a confidence trick (police and general slang).

concealed carry

In the US, the practice of carrying a concealed weapon, usually a **handgun**, is referred to as concealed carry or CCW (carrying a concealed weapon). Some states limit the carrying of a concealed weapon to handguns while others include knives, batons and electronic weapons such as tasers. There is no federal law prohibiting the concealed carrying of weapons and all fifty states permit it in some form.

Concealed Information Test (CIT)

Also known as the Guilty Knowledge Test, this is a method of questioning popular with Japanese **law enforcement** and the **Federal Bureau of Investigation** where a subject is asked a series of questions are asked about a crime, only one of which actually relates to what happened. Its aim is to prove that the subject possesses information only a guilty person would know. The test is normally used alongside a **polygraph test** or **brain fingerprinting**.

concurrent sentence

Sentence of imprisonment that runs at the same time as another sentence, as directed by a court.

connected

Someone who is connected is associated with the **Mafia** or **organised crime** in some way.

consigliere

Advisor to a **Mafia** family who is always consulted before a decision is made.

consumer

In **intelligence** terms, a person or **agency** that uses information or intelligence produced by either its own staff or other agencies.

contamination

In **forensic** terms, the undesirable introduction of substances or trace materials to items which will be subject to forensic examination.

contempt of court

Intentionally obstructing a court in the administration of justice, or acting in a way calculated to lessen its authority or dignity, or failing to obey its lawful **orders**.

controlled substance

Any behaviour-altering or **addictive drug**, such as **heroin** or **cocaine**, the possession and use of which is restricted by law. In the UK these are drugs covered by the 1971 Misuse of Drugs Act, which classifies controlled substances into A, B or C. In the US this is a drug or other substance, or immediate precursor, included in Schedule I, II, III, IV or V of the Controlled Substances Act.

control zone

A controlled airspace extending upwards from the surface of the Earth to a specified upper limit.

conventional force (CF)

This is a force capable of conducting operations using non-nuclear weapons. It can also mean a force other than designated **special operations** forces.

converted firearm

Firearm that has been modified in one or more of its essentials characteristics, e.g. to fire live **bullets** if it formerly fired blanks. Often used in gun crime in the UK to avoid or subvert gun import restrictions.

cooking the books

Making an area appear safer to the general public than it actually is (UK police slang). Also describes an accounting scam.

copycat crime

Crime that has been inspired by prior exposure to a previous crime or media content concerning a crime, including fictional or game content. ▶ **copycat effect** The copycat effect occurs when publicity or media attention around a crime or suicide inspires similar incidents. This is most marked when that media content is sensationalist in nature. The term was first coined c. 1916 when reporting of the **Jack the Ripper** murders inspired copycat killings.

Corinth

Brothel (UK thieves' **cant**, historical slang).

corn

Ammunition or **bullets** (London contemporary gang slang).

coroner

An elected or appointed official who conducts or oversees **investigations** and inquests into the cause and manner of death as well as investigating and confirming the identity of an unknown deceased person. Coroners do not have to be medical professionals and might therefore not be

authorised to conduct autopsies or other invasive procedures themselves. These are the responsibility of a **forensic pathologist**.

Cosa Nostra

Meaning 'our thing', the **Mob** term for a family or the **Mafia**.

cosy mystery

The term 'cosy' ('cozy' in the US) for a mystery or crime
book or series was coined in the late twentieth century
and refers to a genre in which an amateur detective
solves a crime in what is usually a small town or village
setting where an unsuspecting victim has suffered foul
play. The amateur detective is often female and middle-
aged or elderly, highly educated and with a useful
contact in the local police force or **forensic** services.
Supporting these main characters is an array of often
eccentric minor characters and there are plenty of
clues and red herrings to follow. The reader follows
these clues along with the amateur detective but is
often surprised by the identity of the real perpetrator.
Sex and violence are deliberately downplayed in a cosy
mystery and profanity rarely used. The villain is almost
always a member of the same small community within
which the victim lives, or lived, and the murder method
does not involve graphic violence but is unusual or relatively blood free, such as **poisoning**, and takes place
'offstage'. The emphasis in the cosy mystery is on problem and puzzle solving as well as development of the
main characters. They are often written as part of a
series and are hugely popular.

count

In the US, each separate offence, attributed to one or more persons, as listed in a **complaint**, information or indictment.

counterdrug activity

Measure or activity undertaken to detect, disrupt or stop any activity that is reasonably related to illicit **drug trafficking**.

counterespionage (CE)

Counterespionage is the offensive, proactive form of **counterintelligence** and consists of activities designed to gather information about a hostile **intelligence** service using, or attempting to use, that service's own operations.

counterfire

Fire from a ballistic weapon intended to destroy or **neutralise** enemy weapons.

counterguerrilla operation

Activity or operation conducted by security forces against an armed paramilitary wing of an insurgency (guerrillas).

counterintelligence (CI)

Term for activities carried out or information gathered to identify, deceive, thwart, disrupt or otherwise protect against other **intelligence** activities carried out by hostile agencies or governments.

countersurveillance

Actions taken to counteract hostile **surveillance**. Can include systems and techniques designed to detect that surveillance.

counterterrorism

Activities and operations undertaken to **neutralise** terrorists, their organisations and networks in order to stop them using violence to instil fear and to coerce governments or societies so they can achieve their goals.

county lines

Term used in the UK when **drug dealers** from major cities expand their operations to the smaller towns elsewhere, driving out local dealers and exploiting children and vulnerable people to sell their drugs. These children and vulnerable people often have mental health or **addiction** problems and are used to act as drug or money runners so that the dealers behind the operation stay under the radar of **law enforcement**. The dealers take orders for drugs, most commonly **heroin**, crack and **crack cocaine**, over phone lines known as drug lines because they are located some distance from where the drugs are actually delivered. They will sometimes take over a local property, often belonging to a vulnerable person, to aid their operation, and this is known as cuckooing.

court hierarchy UK

The court system in England and Wales is complicated because it has developed over the course of a thousand years. All criminal cases start in a Magistrates' Court. More serious cases will then be committed, or sent, to the Crown Court. From there they may go on to the High Court, possibly the Court of Appeal or eventually the highest court, the Supreme Court. Civil cases may also be heard initially by Magistrates' or County Court. Similarly, they may then end up at the High Court, the Court of Appeal or Supreme Court. In Scotland, most criminal and civil cases are heard initially in Sheriff Courts. Criminal appeals arising from summary criminal proceedings in the Sheriff Courts are heard in the Sheriff Appeal Court. Civil appeals are heard by a bench of three appeal sheriffs sitting in Edinburgh. The Court of Session is the highest court for civil cases while the High Court of Justiciary is the supreme criminal court, hearing the most serious cases such as murder and rape as well as criminal appeals from the High Court.

courtroom drama

The courtroom or legal drama or **thriller** focuses on the legal process, featuring lawyers, jurors, witnesses, defendants and plaintiffs or complainants. At least half the plot or action will take place in the courtroom and may be based on real-life events or be partly or completely fictional. At the heart of the story are the moral dilemmas that are an inevitable part of the legal system and which reflect real life.

cousins

Slang term British **intelligence agents** and operatives use to describe the **Central Intelligence Agency**.

cove

Receiver of stolen goods (UK thieves' **cant**, historical slang).

cover

A cover is a protective measure or series of measures designed to conceal an **agent**, plan, place or operative's true identity and purpose. The term can be applied to anything that masks the true nature of an activity. ▶ **cover legend** A cover legend is a story or scenario designed to provide an agent or operative with an explanation for past and present activities in a way that backs up the cover that has been created for them. ▶ **cover within a cover** If an agent or operative is caught and questioned by hostile forces or **intelligence**, a cover within a cover may be used in which they confess to something lesser than **espionage** in the hope of explaining their suspicious activities.

covert

Way of operating that conceals the identity of the organisation, government or entity that sponsored the operation as well as the relationship of the participants. Covert differs from **clandestine** in that clandestine conceals the nature of the operation itself. ▶ **covert human intelligence source (CHIS)** A CHIS is a police **informant** or, more informally, a snitch or **grass** (UK police acronym).

CQT

See **Comparison Question Test**.

crack cocaine

Crack cocaine is the crystallised form of **cocaine** that is heated and smoked. It comes in solid rocks or blocks and is usually white, pale yellow or rose in colour. The name 'crack' comes from the popping or cracking sound it makes when heated. Crack cocaine is much stronger than regular cocaine, ranging from 75 to 100 per cent pure, and gives users an immediate and powerful high. This effect only lasts for around fifteen minutes and so users will smoke more and more crack to replicate its initial potency. It is one of the most addictive **illegal drugs** currently available with some users developing an **addiction** after just one use. It is also relatively cheap, which means it is readily available but that cost skyrockets as the addict needs to buy ever-increasing quantities to feed their addiction. Crack cocaine has many physical and mental ill-effects and is the root cause of many crimes, including **burglary**, street **theft** and, of course, the manufacture and supply of the drug itself. Also known as apple jacks, badrock, ball, base, beat, candy, chemical, cloud, cookies, crack, crumbs, crunch & munch, devil drug, dice, electric kool-aid, fat bags, French fries, glo, gravel, grit, hail, hard ball, hard rock, hotcakes, ice cube, jelly beans, Kryptonite, nuggets, paste, piece, prime time, product, raw, rock(s), rock star, Rox/Roxanne, scrabble, sleet, snow coke, sugar block, tornado, troop, 24-7.

crackhead

Crack cocaine addict (contemporary slang).

cracking

Cracking is **hacking** a computer system with malicious intent to destroy files, steal personal information such as credit card numbers or data, infect the system with a **virus**, or do many other things that cause harm. ▶ **cracker** A cracker is someone who breaks into a computer system or network without authorisation and with the intention of doing damage. Hackers see themselves as elite programmers who build systems while crackers break them, and are therefore above such activity. Although looked down on by hackers who consider themselves programmers, the two have become synonymous. Cracker derives from 'safecracker' as a way to differentiate it from the various uses of 'hacker' in the cyber world. A cracker may destroy files, steal personal information such as credit card numbers or data, infect the system with a virus, or do many other things that cause harm.

cracksman

Burglar (UK thieves' **cant**, historical slang).

cramp words

Sentence of death passed on a criminal (UK thieves' **cant**, historical slang).

crapped

Executed. ▶ **crapping curl** Executioner (UK thieves' **cant**, historical slang).

crash

To raid or invade (contemporary slang). Also to shoot (London contemporary gang slang associated with drill music). ▶ **crashing corn** Firing a gun (London contemporary gang slang associated with drill music).

crew

Group of 'soldiers' under a **Mafia** officer's command. Also a gang (contemporary slang).

crime scene

A crime scene is any physical place, including a person, building, vehicle or open-air location, that may provide an investigator with **evidence** in the **investigation** of a crime. ▶ **crime scene manager (CSM)** A crime scene manager leads teams of crime-scene investigators and specialists at a complex or major crime investigation scene, ensuring that evidence is collected and preserved in accordance with protocols. They also advise **senior investigating officers** on how to plan **forensic** investigation strategies for crime scenes. ▶ **crime scene reconstruction** The process of determining what actually occurred at a crime scene from an evaluation of physical evidence and other relevant information.

crime scene investigator (CSI)
See **scene of crime examiner**.

criminal damage
Criminal damage occurs when property is intentionally destroyed or damaged, not necessarily to gain entry to premises or a vehicle.

Criminal Investigation Department (CID)
The Criminal Investigation Department of a UK police force, and in those of many former British colonies, is the division to which most plainclothes detectives belong. CID handles incidents such as suspicious death, serious **assault**, **robbery**, **burglary** and major property **theft**, **domestic assault** and racist abuse.

criminalistics
Branch of **forensic** science that involves the examination and interpretation of physical **evidence** in order to aid forensic **investigations**. It includes **crime scene reconstruction**, **drug** analysis, **firearms** and tool marks, fire-debris analysis, molecular biology, photography and trace-evidence analysis.

criminal responsibility, age of
In the UK, children between ten and seventeen can be **arrested** and taken to court if they commit a crime. They are dealt with by youth courts, given different **sentences** to adults and sent to special secure centres for young people, not adult prisons.

critical intelligence

Intelligence that is crucial and requires the immediate attention of the commander or other senior officer.

CSM

See **crime scene manager**.

CSO

See **police community support officer**.

cuffin queer

Magistrate or civil officer in charge of administrating laws. 'Queer' was used in thieves' **cant** for bad or wrong, while 'cuffin' may derive from being smacked on the head rather than handcuffs (UK thieves' **cant**, historical slang).

current standards

Principles of behaviour that exist for the **investigation** of a **case** and can include suspect and witness interviews, documentation of **evidence** and other procedures. In terms of a **cold case**, this means reviewing the case and updating the file and documentation to comply with current standards.

custody

Temporary restraint or detention of a person by lawful authority or process. Also the responsibility for the control, transfer and movement of weapons and components as well as access to them.

cut

Place in prison not covered by **CCTV** cameras so a prisoner 'in the cut' can carry out illicit activity such as **drug** deals (US contemporary prison slang).

cyanide

One of the **poisons** of choice in the Victorian era, particularly as it acted fast, often within minutes. Unfortunately for potential poisoners, its signature effects, which include nausea, vomiting, cardiac arrest, unconsciousness and death, are unmistakable and not easily explained as anything other than murder. From the Second World War onwards, **agents** and operatives in fact and fiction were often supplied with cyanide or 'suicide pills' in case of capture. Serial killer Leonard Lake committed suicide in 1985 using a cyanide pill after his **arrest** for possessing an illegal silencer (**sound moderator**) and **handgun**.

cyber-bullying

Like physical bullying, cyber-bullying is often aimed at children and young people and involves harassing, embarrassing, threatening or humiliating them through their smartphone, computer or tablet; through their social media accounts and in chatrooms; as well as sending harmful, distressing or threatening messages or images via messaging services, email and text. Repeatedly calling a victim's mobile or cell phone is also considered cyber-bullying.

▶ **cyber-stalking/cyber-harassment** Cyber-stalking or cyber-harassment is the term used instead of cyber-bullying when adults are involved.

cybercrime

Use of a computer and a network to carry out illegal acts. These can include using **malware**, ransomware and **botnets**, **hacking** and **cracking**, distributing child pornography, inciting child and **human trafficking**, and for terrorist purposes. Pure cybercrime is that which involves attacks on computer and information systems where the aim is to gain access or to deny legitimate users access. Cyber-enabled crimes include theft, fraud and the distribution of illegal pornography as well as the commissioning of crimes through networks such as the **dark web**. Cybercrime is global, has no borders and is a major source of revenue for **organised crime** as well as terrorist groups. New trends and methods constantly emerge, which makes the policing of it extremely difficult. ▶ **cyberattack** Disruptive or destructive action that targets computer infrastructures, information systems, networks or personal devices. ▶ **cyber weapon** Any software program, **malware**, **Trojan**, **worm** or exploit that is used to attack another system, often one belonging to an enemy nation state or **intelligence agency,** or a major tech, utility or financial institution.

cylinder

Part of a **revolver** holding **rounds** in separate **chambers**. The chambers are sequentially rotated in line with the **barrel** prior to each round being **discharged**.

D

DAC

See **deputy assistant commissioner**.

Dahmer, Jeffrey

Jeffrey Dahmer (1960–94) was an American serial killer
who murdered seventeen mostly African American men
between 1978 and 1991, committing sex acts with their
corpses before dismembering and disposing of them,
although he would often keep their skulls and genitals as
souvenirs. Dahmer was careful to select victims who were
homeless or on the fringes of society and would therefore
be less likely to be missed. He would meet them at bus stops
and in malls and bars, luring them to his home with prom-
ises of money or sex, and giving them **alcohol** laced with
drugs before strangling or bludgeoning them to death. He
liked to take photographs of the stages of his murders and
subsequent dismemberments so he could relive his crimes.
In 1989 Dahmer was convicted of child molestation for
engaging in sexual acts with a thirteen-year-old Laotian
boy and managed to get away with a one-year prison
sentence on day release. In 1991, that same boy's fourteen-
year-old brother was seen running naked down Dahmer's
street and the incident was reported to the police by a
concerned neighbour. The police believed Dahmer when he
told them that the boy was his nineteen-year-old lover and,
after a cursory look at Dahmer's home, left, whereupon he
killed the boy. He went on to kill four more times before

police picked up a thirty-two-year-old African American named Tracy Edwards who was found wandering the streets with handcuffs dangling from his wrist claiming that a 'weird dude' had drugged him. This time, the police decided to investigate and went to Dahmer's home where they found his photographs of his previous killings, along with skulls in the fridge and freezer and jars containing genitalia. Dahmer was **arrested** and subsequently sentenced to sixteen life sentences. He was killed by a fellow prison inmate in 1994. Dahmer inspired an eponymous movie as well as several books.

damages

Money awarded to an individual who has been injured either physically, emotionally or financially through crime. Civil damages are paid in a civil **case**. ▶ **damages, punitive**

Award paid to the injured party that is meant to punish the offender for their actions. ▶ **damages, restorative or compensatory** Award meant to place the injured party in as good a position as they would have been had they not been injured.

dark web, deep web

The dark web is the unindexed part of the World Wide Web that can only be accessed by using the Tor browser. While the pages are public, the IP addresses are hidden and the web sits on darknets, or overlays, on the internet. The dark or deep web is a hive of criminal and illicit activity including trading in stolen information, **drugs**, arms and pornography, but is also used for communication purposes by journalists and people living under oppressive regimes as well as legitimate companies wanting a presence in an arena seen as edgy. Bitcoin initially flourished thanks to the dark web, and vice versa, and is still the major currency used to trade there, along with other cryptocurrencies.

database hit

Link between two or more crimes that results when computer databases connect information or **evidence** from separate crimes or connect physical evidence with a potential suspect.

date rape

Also known as acquaintance **rape**. Date rape specifically refers to a **sexual assault** that occurs during a voluntary social engagement or 'date' where the assailant is known to the victim, who specifically has not consented to and resists the advances. To date rape means to carry out the act as described in the previous definition. ▶ **date-rape drug** A substance used to facilitate a sexual assault, often by incapacitating the victim. Although it is popularly believed that **drugs** such as **GHB** are the most widely used **date-rape** drugs, **alcohol** and **cannabis** are more commonly detected and widely available prescription drugs such as Valium, Xanax and Ambien (zolpidem) are increasingly being used.

Datura stramonium

Also known as jimsonweed, devil's apple, devil's trumpet, thorn apple and locoweed, *Datura stramonium* is a **poisonous** flowering plant from the nightshade family containing hyoscyamine and scopolamine. *Datura* is a deliriant rather than a **hallucinogen**, producing an inability to differentiate reality from fantasy as well as bizarre and sometimes violent behaviour. All parts of the plant are poisonous but especially the seeds and flowers. In some parts of Europe and especially India, where it has been long used in Ayurvedic medicine, *Datura* has also been a popular poison.

Davy's dust
Gunpowder probably derived from the Davy lamp, a miner's safety lamp invented by Sir Humphry Davy in 1815 that helped protect against explosions (UK Victorian slang).

DC
See **detective constable**.

DCC
See **deputy chief constable**.

DCI
See **detective chief inspector**.

DCS
See **detective chief superintendent**.

DEA
See **Drug Enforcement Administration**.

deactivated weapon
A deactivated weapon is a **firearm** that has been modified in such a way that it can no longer **discharge** any **shot**, **bullet** or other missile. Deactivation is intended to be permanent and these weapons should be incapable of being reactivated without specialist tools and skills, although criminals often find a way to do so. The **reactivation** of deactivated weapons and conversion of **blank-firing**

weapons are among the main sources of illegal firearms trafficked in Europe, often coming from eastern Europe and ending up in the UK.

dead drop

A form of **tradecraft** used to pass items, including USB sticks and micro discs, and information between two individuals that does not require them directly to meet or contact one another. The dead drop, also known as a dead-letter box, is a secret location where one party, possibly a **case officer**, leaves the item or information and the other, possibly an **agent** or other officer, collects it and may leave something in return. Once the item has been dropped, a **signal** such as a chalk mark on a lamp-post is left to indicate to the other party that it is ready for collection. Dead-drop locations have included particular stones in parks, wall cavities, bushes and even within the body cavities of dead animals. To prevent the latter from being eaten by predators, both the **Central Intelligence Agency** and KGB came up with the ruse of pouring hot sauce over the carcass.

deadly physical force

In the US this means physical force that can be reasonably expected to cause death or serious physical injury.

deadly weapon

A deadly weapon in the US is one which can cause mortal or great physical harm and usually includes a **firearm** from which a shot can be **discharged**, various knives including switchblades, and metal knuckles.

dead up

Murdered (London contemporary gang slang associated with drill music).

deblurring

Type of image restoration used in **forensics** to reverse image degradation, such as motion blur or out-of-focus blur. It is accomplished by applying algorithms based on knowledge or an estimate of the cause of the original degradation.

degradation

Fragmenting, or breakdown, of **forensic evidence** by chemical, physical or biological means.

deployment

Movement of forces, **agents** or officers into and out of an operational area.

deputy assistant commissioner (DAC)

A deputy assistant commissioner or DAC has a senior management role within the **Metropolitan Police Service** equivalent to that of **deputy chief constable** in other UK police forces. The rank is the fourth highest in the Metropolitan Police Service, between **assistant commissioner** and **commander**.

deputy chief constable (DCC)

Deputy chief constable is the second highest rank in all the territorial police forces in the UK apart from the **Metropolitan Police Service** where the equivalent role is ranked fourth and known as a **deputy assistant commissioner**.

deputy commissioner

'Deputy Commissioner of Police of the Metropolis' is the second highest rank within London's **Metropolitan Police Service** (MPS), ranking below **commissioner** and above **assistant commissioner**.

designer drug

Legally restricted or prohibited **drug** that has been chemically altered to enhance its properties or to circumvent drug laws.

desired point of impact (DPI)

Precise point associated with a target and assigned as the optimal impact point for a single weapon to create a desired effect.

detective chief inspector (DCI)

In the UK, a **chief inspector** who, as a senior detective, is responsible for all local crime **investigation**.

detective chief superintendent (DCS)

Police officer who, in the UK, is the senior detective who usually commands an **investigation** unit or, in the case of the **Metropolitan Police**, a branch of the **Criminal Investigation Department**. The rank is above that of **superintendent** and below that of **chief superintendent**.

detective constable (DC)

A detective constable is a UK police officer who deals with complex and serious **investigations**. DCs have the same rank as **police constables** but do not wear a uniform. Detective constable is the first investigative rank of the

British police forces, below that of **detective sergeant**. Detective constables gather and analyse evidence, talk to witnesses, interview suspects and prepare case files. They work within a **Criminal Investigation Department** or safeguarding units. Since 2017, new recruits have been able to enter the police service at the rank of trainee detective constable. Prior to that, they needed experience of policing in uniform.

detective fiction

A subgenre of crime fiction, classic detective fiction involves an intellectually superior detective or investigator solving an often seemingly perfect crime through a series of deductions, leading to a denouement that often surprises the reader. If the police are involved, they are usually inept. The details of the mystery to be solved and the clues are presented to the reader from the outset so that they may attempt to deduce the identity of the perpetrator alongside the detective.

detective inspector (DI)

A detective inspector is a UK police officer who is responsible for leading complex and serious **investigations**, including those into murder and rape, and ranks above a **detective sergeant**.

detective sergeant (DS)

Rank within the UK police forces that is equivalent to sergeant and ranks below that of **detective inspector**, the prefix 'detective' denoting that the holder has completed at least one detective training course. Detective sergeants are plainclothes officers who investigate major and complex crimes. They may be a member of a **Criminal**

Investigation Department or another investigative unit.

dets

Details of the **investigation** (UK police abbreviation).

deuce and a half

.25mm **automatic firearm** (US contemporary gang slang).

DI

See **detective inspector**.

diamorphine

Diamorphine, otherwise known as **heroin**, is an opioid and strong painkiller that can only be obtained on prescription in the UK. It is not used for medical purposes in the US. Dr **Harold Shipman** (1946–2004), the UK's most prolific serial killer, used 30 mg doses of diamorphine, which is six times greater than the usual amount, to kill his elderly victims who are believed to have numbered at least 218 over twenty-three years.

digital forensics

Digital or **computer forensics** is the application of scientific investigatory techniques to digital and **cybercrimes** and attacks. It involves the collection, preservation, examination and analysis of digital **evidence** using scientifically accepted and validated processes. Digital forensics may be used in the private and public sector, in business and in law, and to solve **cyberattacks** as well as crime.

DILLIGAF

'Do I Look Like I Give a Fuck?' Vulgar term allegedly used by the police and military personnel (UK police and military slang).

dimed

Informed to the police (US/Hispanic contemporary gang slang).

ding wing

Prison psychiatric unit (US contemporary slang).

dinger

Pickpocket or **thief** (UK thieves' **cant**, historical slang).

dip

To stab. ▶ **dipper, dippa, dippaz** Knife, small knife (London contemporary gang slang associated with drill music).

direct evidence

Direct **evidence** is that which directly links a perpetrator to a crime such as an eyewitness account or video footage of the actual crime occurring. If believed, it proves a fact without any need for presumption or inference.

direct fire

Fire delivered on a target using the target itself as the point of aim for either the weapon or the person controlling the weapon.

Directorate of Operations (DO)

The Directorate of Operations, formerly the National Clandestine Service, operates as the **clandestine** arm of the **Central Intelligence Agency**, serving as the 'national authority for the coordination, deconfliction, and evaluation of clandestine **human intelligence** operations across the **Intelligence Community**'. The DO conducts clandestine activities to collect information that cannot be obtained by other means. The DO also conducts **counterintelligence** and special activities as authorised by the US president.

dirty

Drugs (US contemporary gang slang).

discharge

To cause a **firearm** or other weapon to fire.

disguised firearm

Firearm constructed in such a manner that it doesn't look like a firearm. Examples have included guns disguised as pens, mobile phones and torches, all capable of **lethal discharge**.

dissemination

In **intelligence** terms, the delivery of intelligence to users in a suitable form.

DNA (deoxyribonucleic acid)

Molecule that contains the genetic code of human beings and almost all other organisms and which contains the instructions for cell formation. Nearly every cell in a person's body has the same DNA. There are different kinds of DNA that are especially useful to **forensics**.

- Familial DNA: when a routine search of a DNA database has failed to come up with an exact match, a search for familial DNA may be carried out. This is based on the concept that first-order relatives such as a parent, child or sibling will share more DNA than unrelated individuals and so a perpetrator might be tracked down through one of these family members. Jason Ward, the killer of eighty-seven-year-old Gladys Godfrey, was the first murderer to be traced and later convicted through familial DNA in 2003 in Nottinghamshire. It was later used to track down the suspected Golden State Killer in the US, Joseph James DeAngelo (awaiting trial at the time of going to press), as well as solve several **cold cases**.
- mtDNA: mitochondrial DNA exists outside the nucleus of a cell and is inherited from the mother. It does not degrade as much as nuclear DNA and is therefore helpful in identifying **biological material**, such as human remains, that may have degraded. This is therefore particularly helpful in identifying remains that cannot be identified by other means.
- Y-STR DNA: short tandem repeat markers located only on the male Y-chromosome. Useful in cases of **sexual assault** when bodily fluids may need to be identified and separated as belonging to males and females.

DO

See **Directorate of Operations**.

dollymop

Prostitute, often an amateur or part-time working girl (UK Victorian slang).

domestic assault, domestic violence

Sometimes referred to as DA for domestic abuse (UK police and government initialism). Domestic **assault** or violence is defined in the UK as any incident or pattern of incidents of controlling, coercive or threatening behaviour, violence or abuse between those aged sixteen or over who are or have been intimate partners or family members regardless of gender or sexuality. This can encompass but is not limited to psychological, physical, sexual, financial and emotional abuse. Controlling behaviour is defined as a range of acts designed to make a person subordinate and/or dependent by isolating them from sources of support, exploiting their resources and capacities for personal gain, depriving them of the means needed for independence, resistance and escape, and regulating their everyday behaviour. Coercive behaviour is defined as an act or a pattern of acts of assault, threats, humiliation and intimidation or other abuse that is used to harm, punish or frighten the victim.

don

Boss of a gang. The title was originally used by the Sicilian **Mafia** and has now been adopted by many criminals including Jamaican and eastern European gangs.

dose
Burglary (UK thieves' **cant**, historical slang).

dossier
File consisting of information concerning an individual.

dots, dotty
Shotgun (London contemporary gang slang associated with drill music).

double action
Method of firing a gun where a single movement of the **trigger** cocks and releases the **hammer** or **firing pin**.

double agent
Agent in contact with two opposing **intelligence** services, only one of which is aware of the double contact.

double barrel
Two **barrels** in a **firearm** mounted to one frame. The barrels can be aligned vertically, known as **over-and-under**, or horizontally, known as **side-by-side**.

double OG
Second generation of gang members (US contemporary gang slang).

down
To 'go down' is to be sent to prison (UK police and criminal slang).

down and dirty
Police **informant** or selling **drugs** on the side (US contemporary gang slang).

down the brink
Segregated or put in segregation (UK contemporary prison slang).

down with the 5-0
Police **informant** (US contemporary gang slang).

DPI
See **desired point of impact**.

dragsman
Someone who steals from a moving cab or carriage (UK historical slang).

drama
Fight or **assault** (US contemporary prison slang).

draw latch
Burglar, robber of people's houses (UK thieves' **cant**, historical slang).

drawn out
Involved in a gang, committing street crime (London contemporary gang slang associated with drill music).

drip pattern
Bloodstain pattern resulting from a liquid that dripped into another liquid, at least one of which was blood. ▶ **drip stain** A **bloodstain** resulting from a falling drop that formed due to gravity.

drone

After a gunman massacred fifty-eight people at a Las Vegas music festival in 2017, US police have been looking for new ways to heighten event security and they have found an effective method with the use of Unmanned Aerial Systems (UAS), more commonly known as drones. Drones provide a cost-effective way to patrol events, monitor traffic and improve responses to incidents. Police departments also use drones to map fatal car crashes in minutes, when this process used to take hours. In the UK, drones are also used at football matches and events as well as to aid real-time **surveillance**, thanks to visual and thermal imagery, of a suspect police are pursuing. They are also used at protests, **crime scenes** and in disaster zones to aid police operations.

drug

Any substance other than food that, when ingested or otherwise taken into the body, changes the way the body works or the way the person thinks or feels. **Illegal drugs** are those that are proscribed or forbidden under law. The supply of those illegal drugs is big business and often involves **organised crime**, for whom it is the most profitable business model. **Drug trafficking** crosses international borders and jurisdictions, involving national, international and global operations. ▶ **drug abuse** Substance abuse involving the use of illegal drugs or misuse of medicines, which usually follows a pattern in which the user ingests harmful quantities of the substance(s) in question. ▶ **drug culture** Lifestyles of people who abuse drugs, their way of dressing and the behaviour common to abusers of different types of drugs. Also the degree to which drugs pervade so many aspects of society and fundamentally influence culture. ▶**drug dealer** Person who sells illegal drugs. ▶**Drug Enforcement Administration (DEA)** US federal law enforcement **agency** that was established in 1973. The primary task of the agency is to reduce the supply of illegal drugs produced and distributed inside the US or entering the US from abroad. ▶**drug trafficking** Drug trafficking, or the illegal transportation and distribution of illicit substances, is big business on a global scale and infamous as an important source of revenue for **organised crime**. It is also used to finance terrorism. Corruption and ineffective **law enforcement** along the supply chains ensures that drug trafficking continues to flourish. ▶**druggler** Drug dealer (US/Jamaican contemporary gang slang).

drum

House; also to burgle (UK contemporary prison slang).

dry clean

Any technique used to detect and elude **surveillance**. A precaution commonly used by **intelligence officers** and **agents** when actively engaged in an operation.

dubber

Someone who picks locks (UK thieves' **cant**, historical slang).

dummy cartridge

Inert gun **cartridge** designed for **firearms**-handling purposes only, which contains neither **primer** nor **propellant** and cannot be fired under any circumstances. Also known as a dummy **round** or drill round.

dumpster diving

Act of rummaging through the rubbish or trash of an individual or business to gather information that could be useful for identity **theft** or for a cyber criminal to gain access to a system.

dun

Killed or punished (London contemporary gang slang associated with drill music).

duppy

To kill (London contemporary gang slang associated with drill music). Also to mug or beat up (UK contemporary slang).

E

early turn
Police shift or turn of duty starting at 6 a.m. (UK police slang).

echo
Exercise yard (UK contemporary prison slang).

economic espionage
Misappropriation of trade secrets for the benefit of a
foreign government, foreign **agent** or instrument that is an
entity controlled by the government of a foreign country.
Misappropriation includes, but is not limited to, stealing,
copying, altering, destroying, transmitting, sending, receiving, buying, possessing or conspiring to obtain trade
secrets without authorisation.

ECRIS
See **European Criminal Records Information
System**.

edge characteristic
Physical feature of the periphery of a **bloodstain**.

eGuardian
The **Federal Bureau of Investigation**'s sensitive but
unclassified (SBU) terrorism-related threat reporting
system that aids **law enforcement** by allowing them to
rapidly circulate and compare or combine Special Activity

Reports (SARs) that contain information regarding a
potential threat or suspicious activity.

either-way offences

In England and Wales, **indictable offences** are decided as
indictable-only or either-way offences, which means that,
in the case of the latter, the defendant can elect for trial by
jury in a Crown Court or a summary trial in a Magistrates'
Court (see **court hierarchy UK**). That election can be
overruled by the magistrates if they feel that the offence is
too serious for them to hear and that their sentencing
powers would not reflect this seriousness. For some indictable offences, such as **criminal damage** that amounts to a
value of less than £5,000, only summary trial is available.

electronic masking

Controlled radiation of electromagnetic energy to protect the
emissions of communications and electronic systems without significantly degrading the operation of those systems.

electronic tracking device

Tracking device such as a vehicle-locator unit, radio-
frequency beacon or transmitter as well as those devices
that use a Global Positioning System (GPS) or other satellite system for monitoring non-communication activity.

elicitation

In **intelligence** terms, the acquisition of information from
a person or group in a way that does not disclose the intent
or motive behind the interview or conversation.

elimination prints
Finger or handprints taken from people known to have had access to an item examined for **latent prints** so they can be eliminated.

E-man
Prisoner who has tried to escape, been caught and now has to wear an orange sweater or jersey (UK contemporary prison slang).

embezzlement
Financial crime that involves the unlawful misappropriation of funds or assets entrusted to an offender.

Eme
La Eme (Spanish for 'the m') is the Mexican **Mafia**, a highly organised Mexican American criminal gang network based in the US and operating throughout the Californian and federal prison systems among others.

encipher
To convert plain text into unintelligible or **coded** form through the use of a **cipher** system.

EPP
See **Extended sentence for Public Protection**.

espionage
Commonly known as **spying**. **Intelligence** activity that involves the acquisition or **theft** of information through secret or **clandestine** means and which is usually prohibited by the laws of the country in which the espionage is carried out.

European Criminal Records Information System (ECRIS)

The European Criminal Records Information System (ECRIS) was established in April 2012 in order to improve the exchange of information on criminal records throughout the European Union (EU). All EU countries are currently connected to ECRIS. The ECRIS database exchanges information between EU countries on convictions, provides judges and prosecutors with easy access to comprehensive information on the criminal history of the people concerned, including in which EU countries that person has previously been convicted, and removes the opportunity for offenders to escape convictions by moving from one EU country to another.

evidence

Criminal evidence is any **exhibit** or testimony gathered and presented to prove or disprove a crime. There are four basic types of evidence: documentary, testimonial, demonstrative and real. The trial judge decides the **admissibility** of and weight to be given to a piece of evidence within proceedings. **Forensic** evidence is evidence obtained through scientific methods such as **fingerprint** analysis, **DNA** and chemical testing. Evidence tampering is when someone hides, falsifies, destroys or alters evidence to interfere with a criminal **investigation** and is in itself a crime. ▶ **evidence identifier** The tape, labels, containers and string tags used to identify the evidence, the person collecting the evidence, the date the evidence was gathered, basic information about the criminal offence and a brief description of the evidence are all evidence identifiers. ▶ **evidence procedure** Standard put in place for receiving, processing, safeguarding and disposing of physical evidence.

execution warrant

An execution warrant, also known as a death warrant or black warrant, is a writ in the US which authorises someone's execution. An execution warrant is not to be confused with a 'license to kill', which operates like an **arrest** warrant but with deadly force, or the death of subject, instead of arrest as the end goal.

exfiltration

Removal of individuals, operatives or units from areas under enemy control by stealth, deception, surprise or **clandestine** means. It can also mean a clandestine rescue operation intended to remove a defector, refugee or operative and their family from harm or potential harm.

exhibit

Item or **forensic** sample recovered as part of an **investigation**, including but not limited to items found at a **crime scene** such as weapons, **fingerprint lifts**, **casts** of footprints, objects and fibres.

expanding bullet

Bullet designed to extend and expand its surface upon impact with the target.

expiration bloodstain

This is the result of blood being exhaled, coughed out or otherwise released from the mouth. This type of **bloodstain** is often diluted by the presence of saliva or mucous, and the bloodstain forms a characteristic pattern of small, round stains that resemble a fine mist.

explosive cargo

Material such as **ammunition**, bombs, depth charges, demolition material, rockets and missiles in the process of being transported.

explosive hazard

Any material posing a potential threat that contains an explosive component such as unexploded explosives, booby traps, improvised explosive devices (IEDs) and bulk explosives.

Extended sentence for Public Protection (EPP)

Extended **sentence** for Public Protection, also known as a 'section 227 or 228' extended sentence. These were sentences that were introduced in the UK in April 2005 and replaced in 2012 by the Extended Determinate Sentence.

extortion

Extortion is to unlawfully obtain money, property or any other thing of value either tangible or intangible through the use or threat of force, misuse of authority, threat of criminal prosecution, threat of destruction of reputation or social standing, or through other coercive means.

extractor mark

Also known as an ejector mark. This is a mark created on a gun **cartridge case** by the metal-to-metal contact between the cartridge case and the extractor and ejector mechanisms in the weapon. The extractor mechanism removes a cartridge from the **chamber**, while the ejector throws the cartridge away once it is extracted. **Revolvers** do not have ejectors, but **automatic** and **semi-automatic** weapons such as **pistols** and **rifles** do. As a result, the cartridge cases used in these weapons are designed differently from **ammunition** used in revolvers.

eyewash

False entries made in files by **clandestine agents** and officers to protect the security of a **source**.

F

facial recognition

A facial recognition system is one that can recognise some-one from a digital source such as a photograph or video. Controversially used by the police and **law enforcement** at events and protests to identify known perpetrators or simply participants.

facial reconstruction

Facial reconstruction is a **forensic anthropology** technique used when a victim's remains are unidentifiable, usually because they are skeletal or near skeletal. The reconstruction may be two-dimensional, based on photographs of the skull, or three-dimensional either based on sculptures created with modelling clay and other materials or on high resolution 3D computer images. The F.A.C.E. and C.A.R.E.S. computer programs assist in creating faster 2D facial reconstructions while both methods normally require an artist and a forensic anthropologist. Forensic facial reconstructions are controversial and are not a legally recognised technique for positive identification or **admissible** as expert testimony in the US, England and Wales.

fall guy

Someone who takes the blame to protect other people, often other members of a gang (US historical slang).

false flag recruitment

This is when an **intelligence** service recruits someone who believes that they are cooperating with representatives of a specific country or entity, when actually they have been deceived and are cooperating with an intelligence service of another country or entity altogether. The action of the **agent** who recruits them is known as a 'false flag approach'.

family liaison officer (FLO)

Officer who is assigned to a family who are the victims of serious crimes such as abduction and murder.

Faraday bag

Special **forensic** collection bag for electronic parts with a lining that protects the contents from electromagnetic forces.

farmero

A member of the *Nuestra Familia*, a prison gang based in the US (US/Hispanic prison gang slang).

fatacc

Fatal accident (UK police acronym).

FBI

See **Federal Bureau of Investigation**.

FCIP

See **Foreign Counterintelligence Program**.

Federal Bureau of Investigation (FBI)

The Federal Bureau of Investigation, headquartered in Washington, DC, is the principal federal **law enforcement**

agency of the United States and its domestic **intelligence** and **security service**. It is comparable in some areas of its national operations to **MI5** in the UK and, as well as operating across the US, it also maintains offices in US embassies and consulates around the world. Despite its domestic focus, the FBI can and does carry out **clandestine** activities overseas, usually in conjunction with foreign security services and in joint operations with other agencies such as the **Central Intelligence Agency**, although there is famously rivalry between the two. The FBI has featured in numerous books, films and TV series since the 1930s including *The X-Files* (1993–2018).

felony

In the United States, a felony is the most serious type of criminal offence and typically involves serious physical harm, or threat of harm, to victims. Felony offences also include white-collar crimes and **fraud** schemes. Offences that would otherwise be counted as **misdemeanours** can be elevated to felonies for second-time offenders. Punishment for felonies ranges from imprisonment for one year to life in prison without **parole**. Felonies such as murder may even be punished by imposition of the death penalty.

fence

Receiver of stolen goods (UK thieves' **cant**, historical slang still in contemporary use).

fence kenn

House where stolen goods are kept (UK thieves' **cant**, historical slang).

fentanyl

Fentanyl, a **synthetic** opioid, is the leading cause of **drug** overdoses in the US. Much more powerful than **heroin**, fentanyl is often added to it, which results in a **lethal** combination. A single tablespoon of fentanyl could kill up to five hundred people, which is why **Drug Enforcement Agents** take precautions not to touch or inhale the drug and often carry the antidote Narcan (naloxone) to reverse its effects. There are concerns that fentanyl could be used as a weapon of terror or mass destruction. More deaths result from its misuse than from car accidents in the US. Street names include: Apache; *birria* (fentanyl mixed with heroin); blonde; blue diamond; blue dolphin; blues; butter; China girl; China Town; China white; Chinese; Chinese buffet; Chinese food; crazy; crazy one; dance fever; dragon; dragon's breath; F; food; Freddy; fuf (furanyl fentanyl); Facebook (fentanyl mixed with heroin in pill form); fent; fenty; fire; friend; girl; goodfella; great bear; grey stuff; He-Man; Heineken; *huerfanito*; humid; jackpot; King Ivory; lollipop; Murder 8; nal; nil; nyl; opes; pharmacy; poison; shoes; snowflake; tango and cash; TNT; toe tag dope; white girl; white ladies.

FI

See **foreign intelligence**.

figure

Boy small enough to squeeze through an open window who then hands stolen goods to his **accomplice** outside or below (UK thieves' **cant**, historical slang).

figure   127

filch

To steal (thieves' **cant**, historical slang UK still used as contemporary slang).

Financial Crimes Enforcement Network (FinCEN)

FinCEN safeguards the US financial system from financial crime, including terrorist financing, **money laundering** and other illicit activity. FinCEN aids **law enforcement**, **intelligence** and regulatory agencies by sharing and analysing financial intelligence, and works globally, cooperating with counterpart foreign **financial intelligence units**, networks and people.

financial intelligence unit (FIU)

Each member of the EU must have a national financial intelligence unit, which receives, analyses and disseminates information gathered from **Suspicious Activity Reports**. The UKFIU is based within the **National Crime Agency**.

FinCEN

See **Financial Crimes Enforcement Network**.

fingerprint

Impression of the friction ridges of all or any part of the finger.

FIO

See **foreign intelligence officer**.

fire

Police approaching (US/Jamaican contemporary gang slang).

firearm

Lethal barrelled weapon that uses the combustion of a **propellant** to launch one or multiple **projectiles**, usually **bullets** or **pellets**, or to produce a sound or flash effect. Also called a weapon, gun, **handgun**, **pistol**, **revolver**, etc.
▶ **firearms identification** The application of **forensic** science to determine if a bullet, **cartridge case** or other **ammunition** was fired in a particular firearm to the exclusion of all others.

fired standard

Component of a collection and catalogue of test-fired **bullets**, **cartridge cases** and **shot** shells from known **firearms** kept in a **forensics** laboratory. Also called known standards, **ammunition** standards or reference ammunition.

firing pin

Part of a **firearm** that strikes the **ammunition primer** or the rim of the **cartridge**, igniting the **propellant** and discharging the **projectiles**.

first responder

First police, ambulance or other officer arriving at a **crime scene**, who is responsible for the immediate action taken at that scene including the preservation of human life and, in the case of **law enforcement**, crime-scene examination. Their responsibility ends when the officer with official responsibility for the crime scene takes over. Also known as the first intervener.

F

fish

New and usually naive prisoner who is educated in the ways of prison life by other inmates (US contemporary prison slang).

FIU

See **financial intelligence unit**.

flaps and seals

Intelligence term for the **clandestine** or secret opening, reading and resealing of envelopes or packages without the recipient's knowledge.

flat joint worker

Someone who assists in a gambling scam (US historical slang).

flat worker

Someone who steals from homes and apartments (US historical slang).

flicky

Flick-knife (London contemporary gang slang associated with drill music).

FLO

See **family liaison officer**.

flow pattern

Bloodstain pattern resulting from the movement of a volume of blood on a surface due to gravity or the movement of the target.

fluorescence

Fluorescence is the use of a particular light waveband to cause a substance to illuminate and is used in the **forensic** examination of **crime scenes** and materials. Different wavebands cause different substances or materials to fluoresce. UV light is used to detect body fluids and **drug** residues while blue or violet light causes some human and animal hair as well as body fluids to glow. UV and blue light are also used for **fingerprints**. Blue/green light is used to detect **gunshot residue**, accelerants and explosives. ▶**fluorescent powders** Powders that contain fluorescent chemicals, which reveal **latent prints** under an **alternate light source**.

FMJ

See **full metal jacket**.

food

Drugs (London contemporary gang slang associated with drill music).

footpad

Highwayman, **thief** or robber who went on foot and stole from pedestrians. Footpads operated from the sixteenth century to the nineteenth, when the term fell out of use. They were considered to be common thieves and the lowest form, with highwaymen being considerably more glamorised and, in some cases, gaining fame or notoriety (UK thieves' **cant**, historical slang).

Foreign Counterintelligence Program (FCIP)

The military division of the US National Intelligence Program (NIP) that conducts **counterintelligence** activities in support of the US Department of Defense.

foreign intelligence (FI)

Intelligence or information about the intentions, capabilities and activities of foreign powers, organisation or people. It does not include **counterintelligence** except for information on international terrorist activities. ▶**foreign intelligence officer (FIO)** Member of a foreign intelligence service.

forensics

Forensics are scientific methods or techniques used in the detection or **investigation** of a crime. The term can also be used informally to refer to the laboratory or department where these tests are conducted. ▶**forensically clean** When applied to **digital forensics**, digital media that are completely wiped of nonessential and residual data, scanned for **viruses** and verified before use. ▶**forensic anthropology** Application of anthropological methods and theory, particularly those relating to the recovery and analysis of human remains, to help solve crime. ▶**forensic crime fiction** Subgenre of crime fiction that centres on the work of **medical examiners** and pathologists. In this genre the forensic expert takes on the role of the investigator and solves the crime by scientifically examining the clues left on the body or at the **crime scene**. ▶**forensic entomology** Study and analysis of insects and arthropods to aid investigations, especially where cadavers are concerned. The developmental stages of the insect or arthropod in a decomposing body can offer a wealth of information to investigators. ▶**forensic examiner** Someone who conducts and/or directs the analysis of **evidence**, interprets the data and reaches conclusions. ▶**forensic genealogy** Combined use of family histories and partial **DNA** matches to identify the likely donor of a

DNA sample. The GEDmatch database in Florida is an open data personal genomics and genealogy database that helped to identify the suspected Golden State Killer.

▶**forensic odontology** Dentistry dealing with the proper handling and examination of dental **evidence** and the proper evaluation, interpretation and presentation of such evidence in the interest of the law. A forensic odontologist deals with the identification of unknown human remains through dental records; assists at scenes of mass disaster; estimates the age of living and dead people; analyses bitemarks found on victims, other evidence and various materials; and presents that evidence in court. They can also analyse weapon marks using the principles of analysis for **bitemark identification**. ▶**forensic pathology** Determination of the cause of death through the examination of a corpse. A forensic pathologist who has specialised medical and forensic training will carry out a post-mortem or **autopsy** to determine the cause of death, acting as a medical expert for justice. ▶**forensic toxicology** Gathering, identifying and evaluating evidence relating to **drugs** and **poisons** to aid criminal investigations or legal proceedings. Forensic toxicologists are often senior and highly experienced toxicologists, or experts on the harmful effects of chemicals on humans, and use techniques such as analytical chemistry to isolate, identify and quantify drugs and poisonous substances in forensic samples. They consider all kinds of factors such as chemical metabolism and how that can affect concentration or **toxic** effects as well as drug interactions, tolerance, post-mortem redistribution and the differences between people that have an effect such as age, height, weight and medical history. Forensic toxicologists are often called upon as expert witnesses and to give an expert opinion as to whether a particular substance could have proved toxic or even fatal.

▶ **forensic wipe** Verifiable procedure for sanitising a defined area of digital media by overwriting each byte with a known value.

for helvede

Danish vulgar slang comparable to 'for fuck's sake', a phrase that often appears in **Scandi noir**.

forward spatter pattern

Bloodstain pattern resulting from blood drops that travelled in the same direction as the impact force.

fraud

Fraud occurs when a person criminally or wrongfully deceives another for the purposes of personal or financial gain or to deprive them of a legal right. Fraud may be a civil or criminal offence depending on the circumstances.

fröken, frøken

Fröken is the Swedish and *frøken* the Danish and Norwegian for 'Miss', a respectful title for a young, unmarried woman or teacher. The word often appears in **Scandi noir**.

front

Someone without a criminal record who acts as the public-facing person for a known criminal who is the real owner of a club or business. Also an apparently legitimate business operation that conceals the real, illegal business operating on its premises or under its aegis.

fugu

Fugu, the name given to the Japanese pufferfish and the **poison** it contains (tetrodotoxin), is deadlier than **cyanide**, paralysing and then suffocating the unfortunate victim who remains conscious to the end. When prepared properly, fugu poses little risk but every year in Japan around fifty poisonings occur, although they are rarely fatal thanks to extensive knowledge of the symptoms. James Melville used fugu poisoning as a murder weapon in his fifth Inspector Otani novel, *Sayonara Sweet Amaryllis*, while James Bond survived a near fatal dose of fugu in *Dr No*.

full

Arrest (US historical slang).

full metal jacket (FMJ)

Projectile in which the **bullet jacket** encloses most of the core, with the exception of the base (see **total metal jacket**). Also known as full jacketed, full patch and full metal case.

G

G

A grand or a thousand dollars in **Mafia** and other gang slang.

Gacy, John Wayne

John Wayne Gacy was an American serial killer who was known as the Killer Clown because he would dress as Pogo or Patches the clown to entertain children at charitable events. Gacy **raped**, tortured and murdered at least thirty-three young men and boys between 1972 and 1978. Born in 1942 in Illinois, Gacy committed his first known offence in 1967, sexually **assaulting** a fifteen-year-old boy for which he was **sentenced** to ten years in prison. Released after eighteen months on **parole**, Gacy sexually assaulted another teenage boy in 1971 but the boy failed to appear in court and the **case** was dropped. Gacy then bought a house in Cook County, Illinois, with help from his mother and it was at this house that all his subsequent murders were committed. He married his second wife in 1972, at which point his mother moved out of the house. He told his wife he was bisexual in 1975 and that they would not be having sex again. That year, after his wife saw him bringing teenage boys to their garage and found gay pornography in the house, she petitioned for divorce. After she also moved out in 1976, Gacy ramped up his activity during what he referred to as his 'cruising years', and the majority of his murders were committed between then and 1978. After the disappearance of fifteen-year-old Robert Piest, who had last been seen speaking with Gacy about a possible job, police placed Gacy under **surveillance**, having also learned about his previous conviction. Gacy became so affable with the detectives on the surveillance team that he invited them out for meals, remarking over breakfast with them, 'You know . . . clowns can get away with murder.' After he then invited these same detectives into his house, one noticed a smell that was similar to that of a rotting corpse. This, along with testimony from two of his victims who had survived, was enough to convince the police to apply for a second **search warrant** for Gacy's house. Gacy, in the interim, confessed all to his lawyer and then to police who confronted him with the fact they had found bodies in the crawl space in his house. Gacy stood trial in 1980 and was sentenced to death. He served fourteen years on death row and, after his final **appeal** was rejected, was executed on 9 May 1994. His brain was removed after he was declared dead and remains in the possession of Helen Morris, who was a witness for the defence and conducts research into violent sociopaths. Several of Gacy's victims remain unidentified and his crimes helped inspire the Missing Children Act of 1984, which led directly to the **AMBER alert** system in use all over the world today. Many on the **investigation** team believe he did not act alone but had at least one **accomplice**, a fact borne out by witness testimony. Gacy himself claimed that there were others who aided him in his crimes and also committed them, but no accomplice has ever been found or brought to justice.

gang banger

Gang member or gang activity. ▶ **gang banging** Gang activity (US contemporary gang slang).

ganja baron

Major **drug** smuggler (US/Jamaican contemporary slang).

gap

In **spy** jargon, 'in the gap' means being free of **surveillance** for a few seconds but not as long as a minute.

garbage business

Euphemism for **organised crime**, so-called because one universally popular gangster business is waste disposal. In New York City the ***Cosa Nostra*** dominated the trash collection industry from the 1950s until Mayor Rudy Giuliani seized control of it in the 1990s. The construction industry was also infamously dominated by the US **Mafia**. Worldwide, the practice still continues although larger organised crime operations focus on more profitable sectors such as **drug trafficking** and **human trafficking**.

garnish

Money demanded of, and paid by, prisoners to their fellow inmates on their admittance to prison (UK thieves' **cant**, historical slang).

gas firearm

Object or device that may or may not have the appearance of a **firearm**, originally designed and intended to produce only a gas expulsion and whose characteristics exclude the firing of any other **projectile**. Normally the **cartridges** are filled with a noxious substance such CS gas to temporarily disable an attacker. Gas firearms are often **converted** in the course of illicit gun trafficking so that they can be used as **lethal** weapons. ▶ **gas-operated firearm** Fully **automatic** or **semi-automatic firearm** in which the **propellant** gases are used to unlock the breech bolt and then to complete the cycle of extraction and ejection. This is accomplished usually in conjunction with a spring, which returns the operating parts to battery. Gas-operated firearms are popular with the military.

G

gate fever

Excitement or emotion shown by a prisoner nearing the end of their **sentence** (UK contemporary slang).

gateway drug

Drug, usually a **controlled substance**, that when used may lead to the use of more **addictive** substances.

gauge

Term used to denote the **calibre** of a **shotgun**. It is taken as a measure of the number of identical solid spheres, of the same diameter as the bore of the smooth **barrel**, that can be made from a pound of lead (so the twelve identical solid spheres that can be made from a pound of lead fit the internal diameter of a twelve-bore shotgun).

GBH

See **grievous bodily harm**.

Gein, Ed

Ed Gein was an American serial killer and the inspiration for both *Psycho* (1960) and *The Silence of the Lambs* (1991) as well as Leatherface in *The Texas Chain Saw Massacre*

(1974). Born in 1906 in Wisconsin, Gein was dominated by his deeply religious mother Augusta, who ruled their repressive household and constantly warned Ed and his brother Henry about the sins of lust and carnal desire. Ed rarely left the farm, especially after his **alcoholic** father died and his brother Henry perished in mysterious circumstances in a fire. Subsequently, Ed became more and more devoted to his mother, never dating or leaving the farm, and after she too died in 1945, he kept her room absolutely pristine while the rest of the house fell into squalor. Although several people in the neighbourhood disappeared over the years, it was only when the local hardware store owner also disappeared, leaving a trail of blood that led out the back of her shop, that her son, the deputy sheriff who was already suspicious of the reclusive Gein, apprehended him. When officers went to his farmhouse they were greeted by the sight of the headless, gutted body of Beatrice Worden hanging from the ceiling. During their subsequent search they discovered skulls of other victims fashioned into soup bowls and body organs in jars. Under questioning, Gein admitted to the murder of Worden and another local woman, Mary Hogan, three years earlier, as well as digging up bodies to cut off body parts, wearing suits and masks he had made out of human skin, and necrophilia, among other gruesome practices. The mild-mannered Gein was found to be insane and unfit to stand trial and was committed. Nine years later, he was found fit to stand trial but was judged insane at the time of Worden and Hogan's murders and recommitted to the Central State Hospital, where he died of cancer in 1984 at the age of seventy-seven.

get down

Fight (US contemporary gang slang).

GHB

GHB (*gamma*-Hydroxybutyric acid) is a popular **date-rape drug**, starting to act within fifteen minutes of administration, and has until recently been notoriously difficult to detect thanks to its rapid metabolisation by the body. New techniques that involve Nuclear Magnetic Resonance (NMR) Spectroscopy now mean that GHB **metabolites** can be detected up to twenty-four hours later in the body, with techniques still being perfected that allow its detection up to a month or more after ingestion in the victim's hair. Street names include: blowout; Bruno Mars; cherry meth; easy lay; everclear; fantasy; G; gamma oh; GEEB; Georgia home boy; goop; great hormones at bedtime; grievous bodily harm; G-riffic; Gina; jib; liquid E; liquid X; monkey juice; organic Quaalude; salty water; scoop; soap; water.

ghost

To move a prisoner without warning from one prison to another. Also 'to be ghosted' is find a visitor has not turned up at the visitor's centre (UK contemporary prison slang).

giallo

Twentieth-century genre of Italian literature and film that encompasses crime fiction, **thrillers** (often **psychological**), mystery and horror. *Giallo* means yellow, reflecting the colour of cheap paperback mystery novels in post-war Italy.

Glasgow smile

Popular among Scottish gangs in the 1920s and 1930s, a Glasgow smile describes two characteristic slashes or cuts from the corners of the mouth to the ears, which result in scars giving the victim the appearance of a perpetual smile or grin. It is also known as a Chelsea smile, due to its popularity with a gang known as the Chelsea Headhunters, or a Glasgow, Chelsea, Cheshire or Birkenhead grin. Elizabeth Short, the murder victim known posthumously as the Black Dahlia, was subjected to mutilation including a Glasgow smile.

Glavnoye Razvedyvatel'noye Upravlenie (GU)

Commonly known by its previous abbreviation GRU, this is the Main Directorate of the General Staff of the Armed Forces of the Russian Federation aka Russian military **intelligence**. It is believed to have a far larger **spy** network abroad than Russia's **foreign intelligence** service.

glazier

Person who breaks a shop window in order to steal the goods within (UK thieves' **cant**, historical slang).

Glock

Austrian manufacturer of **handguns**. ▶ **Glock 17** 9 mm **pistol** which is the most popular handgun for the military and **law enforcement** agencies in the world and is the gun most commonly issued to police **firearms** officers in the UK. It is popular due to its rugged polymer build, accuracy and safety features, which mean it is unlikely to accidentally **discharge**. ▶ **Glock 19** 9mm pistol issued to West Midlands police officers in the UK as an alternative to the Glock 17. It is a compact version of the Glock 17 and was developed by the manufacturer specifically for the military and law enforcement. ▶ **Glock 22** The Glock 17's cousin, modified to take fifteen **rounds** of .40 **calibre ammunition** while still being light enough to comfortably carry all day. The G22 is used by several law enforcement agencies, including US Marshals, the **Drug Enforcement Administration** and the **Federal Bureau of Investigation**, and is the most popular police service pistol in the US. ▶ **Glock 26** Subcompact 9 mm pistol designed for **concealed carry** and is issued to plainclothes officers in London's **Metropolitan Police**. Like all Glock pistols, it is made from polymer, which means it is both light and durable.

G

going postal
Going to a pre-planned fight, usually gang-related (UK contemporary slang). Also running amok and shooting colleagues in the workplace, named after shootings by US Postal Service workers.

golden hour
The hour between 8 and 9 a.m. when prisoners fill out applications (apps) for various requests such as to make phone calls (UK contemporary prison slang, originally local to HMP Winchester).

gong
Gun (US/Jamaican contemporary gang slang).

good fellow
'Honest' **thief** who is generous and settles bills on time (US historical slang).

got
Assaulted or robbed (London contemporary gang slang associated with drill music).

gov, guv, guv'nor

Prison officer or senior police officer (UK contemporary prison and police slang).

grandma's house

Gang headquarters or meeting place in a prison or the **cell** of the gang leader (US contemporary prison slang).

grass

Snitch or **informer**. Also to grass or grass someone up means to inform on them or snitch (UK contemporary police and general slang).

Greater Manchester Police (GMP)

British police force sometimes referred to as the GMP (UK police acronym).

green-goods man

Someone who deals in forged currency or bonds (US historical slang).

Grey List

List of the identities and locations of people of interest whose attitudes or political inclinations towards the US and its policies are unclear or unknown. Those people may possess information or particular skills required by US forces and whose political motivations or attitudes require further **investigation** before the US can attempt to make use of that information and/or skills. (See also **Black List** and **White List**.)

G-ride

Gangster ride or stolen car (US contemporary gang slang).

Griess Test

Chemical test that detects nitrites and is used to develop patterns of **gunpowder** residues, which are nitrites, around **bullet** holes.

grievous bodily harm (GBH)

Assault causing grievous bodily harm (GBH) is assault or battery that causes serious physical harm to the victim, such as stabbing them. If there is no serious harm then an offence of wounding with intent will have been committed. If there is intent to cause serious harm then the offence of GBH becomes greater and is **charged** under Section 18, which can result in a life **sentence**.

grifter

Con artist or trickster who **swindles** money out of people through what is usually small-scale, petty **fraud**. Also known as a scammers, gougers, chisellers and flim-flam men. The term originated in around 1906 in circuses and carnivals where grifters operated sideshows, often with a gambling element dishonestly fixed in their favour. Its use has been extended to all non-violent criminals (US slang).

grip

Handle of a **handgun** and portion of the **stock** to the rear of the **trigger** on a long gun.

groaner

Person who was employed to attend church services and meetings to sigh appreciatively or look demure while at the same time picking the pockets of the congregation and stealing watches, prayer books and anything else they could get their hands on (UK thieves' **cant**, historical slang).

groove

Spiral or helicoidal cut in a gun **barrel**, which creates the **rifling** that is important in **forensic ballistics**. These grooves impart spin to the **bullet** or projectile on firing. A spinning bullet is more stable in its trajectory and therefore more accurate than one fired from a **smooth-bored** weapon.

grow house

A grow house or **cannabis** farm is an often innocuous-looking house where thousands of cannabis plants might be grown in every room, sometimes tended by illegal immigrants. The **drug** gangs who run these farms will hack into the electricity supply to avoid having to pay the enormous bills that result from running the lights, heaters and hydroponic systems necessary to cultivate their crop.

GRU

See *Glavnoye Razvedyvatel'noye Upravlenie*.

GSR

See **gunshot residue**.

GTP

'Good To Police': the unethical practice of shops, clubs, bars and other businesses and individuals supplying goods and services free to police officers in return for favours such as being tipped off when a raid might be conducted or turning a blind eye when necessary. Officially this is corruption and never happens. Unofficially, officers will allegedly tell one another which local suppliers and businesses are 'good to police' (UK contemporary police slang).

GU

See *Glavnoye Razvedyvatel'noye Upravlenie*.

gump

Gay male prisoner (US contemporary prison slang).

gun

Common term for a **firearm**, for example, a **handgun** or **rifle**.

gun moll

Female **pickpocket** (US historical slang).

gunpowder

Generic term for **cartridge** and **muzzle**-loading **propellant**.

gunshot residue (GSR)

Residues from the powder, **primer** and **projectile**, as well as from the metallic components of the **cartridge case** and **firearm**'s **barrel**, which are partly expelled from the firearm during firing and partly remain in the firearm, mainly in the bore. Can be important to **forensic evidence** and **investigation**.

G

H

hacking

Hacking is the act of gaining access to a computer system by exploiting vulnerabilities in that system. ▶ **hacker** Person who gains unwarranted access to a computer system. Hackers contend that they are problem solvers who reveal bugs and flaws in a system and alert companies to vulnerabilities so that they can be fixed. They consider themselves highly skilled and capable of thinking outside the box, looking down on **crackers** who break into computer systems for illegal purposes or personal gain.

half cock

Safety notch on a gun meant to prevent shocks or decocking; the intermediary position of the **hammer** between the notch of the armed and decocking positions intended to prevent release of the hammer without pressing on the **trigger**. This is the safety or loading position of many guns.

hallucinogen

Substance, especially a psychoactive **drug** such as **lysergic acid diethylamide** (LSD), phencyclidine (**PCP**) or **ketamine**, that causes hallucinations, altering perception, experience and feeling. Hallucinogens are also known as dissociatives and are usually **controlled substances** in the UK and the US. While not highly **addictive**, they can be fatally dangerous and are often misused.

hammer

Part of the firing mechanism on a gun which strikes the **firing pin**, **primer** or percussion cap. In some cases the firing pin is an integral part of the hammer.

handgun

Firearm designed to be held and fired in one hand rather than being shouldered.

handler

Intelligence officer directly responsible for the operational activities of an **agent**. Also known as an agent handler or **case officer**.

handloading

Manually assembling a gun **cartridge case** with a **primer**, **propellant** and **bullet** or **wadding** and **shot**.

hand ting

Pistol or **handgun** (London contemporary gang slang associated with drill music).

happy bag

Bag armed robbers use that contains the weapons, balaclavas, gloves and other equipment required to carry out robberies.

hard-boiled crime fiction

The lone-wolf PI skulking behind a frosted office door is the stuff of hard-boiled fiction. Usually American, tough-talking and tough-acting, he (it is always a 'he' in hard-boiled crime fiction) is a pro, an unsentimental gunslinger for hire. And the person who hires him is often a woman in distress. These flawed heroes march alone against a corrupt society, taking on the system while adhering to their skewed personal code of honour. Always moral, they won't be cowed or beaten and they never give up on a client or a **case**. Classic exponents of the art include Dashiell Hammett and Raymond Chandler. Their contemporary successors include James Ellroy, Michael Connelly and Dennis Lehane. These authors may not always write about a PI but their prose echoes the classic tropes and their heroes remain slang-slinging modern-day men of myth who take on the world and shoot from the lip.

hate crime

Hate crime is defined in the UK as 'any criminal offence which is perceived, by the victim or any other person, to be motivated by hostility or prejudice towards someone based on a personal characteristic'. There are five centrally monitored strands, which are hate crime based on race or ethnicity, religion or beliefs, sexual orientation, disability and transgender identity.

HDC
See **home detention curfew**.

headtopped
Shot in the head (London contemporary gang slang associated with drill music).

heave

Rob. ▶**heave the booth** Rob someone's house (UK thieves' **cant**, historical slang).

heavy weapon

Weapon intended to be used by more than one member of armed or security forces, as a team, and whose **calibre** is bigger or equal to 100 mm. According to NATO definitions, the term 'heavy weapons' means all tanks and armoured vehicles, all artillery 75 mm calibre and above, all mortars 81 mm calibre and above, and all anti-aircraft weapons 20 mm calibre and above.

hebephile

Someone who is primarily attracted to adolescents or post-pubertal teenagers who are still in the early stages of sexual maturation, i.e. usually between eleven and fourteen years of age (those attracted to older teenagers are called ephebo-philes). Hebephiles are usually solely sexually attracted to these adolescents and do not pursue sexual relationships with adults. As such, they often put themselves in profes-sional and other roles where they have easy access to their vulnerable targets.

Heckler & Koch MP5

The Heckler & Koch MP5 is a range of lightweight, delayed blowback **sub-machine guns**, with the MP5SF model used by various UK police forces including the **Metropolitan Police**. The MP5SD silenced version of the gun was specifically developed by its German manufactur-ers for use by special forces.

heel

Rear portion of a **bullet**.

Helicopter Emergency Medical Service (HEMS)

Helicopter Emergency Medical Services, often funded by charities, provide rapid aerial response to a medical emergency.

hemlock

One of the most **poisonous** plants in the world, hemlock (*Conium maculatum*) grows readily in the wild as well as in gardens and, before its tiny white flowers appear, is sometimes mistaken for parsley or carrot leaves. Hemlock poisoning results in total paralysis followed by death due to asphyxiation, although the mind remains unaffected, which means the victim is fully aware of what is happening. It takes only a few drops of liquid hemlock to kill a small animal and a **lethal** dose for a human of prepared hemlock is estimated at around 100 mg. Socrates, the Greek philosopher, was **sentenced** to death by drinking hemlock, sparking the imagination of Shakespeare and other writers who seized upon this as a murder method in fiction.

hempen furniture

Blood money or money received for delivering up felons. It derives its name from the fact that a hangman's noose was made from hemp (UK thieves' **cant**, historical slang).

hempen widow

Woman whose husband has been hanged. It derives its name from the fact that a hangman's noose was made from hemp (UK thieves' **cant**, historical slang).

HEMS

See **Helicopter Emergency Medical Service**.

henbane

Henbane (*Hyoscyamus niger*) is a plant, the flowers of
which are so **poisonous** that smelling them causes giddi-
ness. It contains the tropane alkaloids hyoscine (scopolamine), hyoscyamine and **atropine**. Among its many symptoms are a dry mouth, blurred vision, photophobia,
vomiting, confusion, hallucinations, convulsions and coma.
It was infamously used by Dr Crippen to murder his wife
although most modern poisonings are the accidental result
of overdose after ingesting henbane as a **hallucinogen**.

heroin

Heroin is a highly **addictive** opioid, also known as diamorphine, and is usually sold as a brown or white powder that is
smoked, snorted or dissolved in liquid and injected. When
smoked it is often heated on a surface such as tinfoil with
the resultant smoke inhaled. This is known as 'chasing the
dragon'. It is very easy to overdose on heroin, especially
when it is injected, and overdose often results in death from
either inhaling vomit or the slowing of breathing to the
point where it stops. In the US, where deaths due to **drugs**
and especially opiates outnumber deaths due to gun
violence, a crime-fiction genre known as Opioid Noir has
flourished since Hammett and Chandler highlighted the
growing post-war drug crisis, with recent writers such as
James Ellroy, James Lee Burke and Don Winslow also shin-
ing a light on the opioid epidemic. Heroin's street names
include: abajo; A-bomb (heroin mixed with **cannabis**);
achivia; adormidera; amarilla; *anestesia de caballo* (heroin
mixed with the horse anaesthetic xylazine); antifreeze;

apodo; arpon; Aunt Hazel; avocado; azucar; bad seed; *baja corte* (diluted heroin); ballot; basketball; basura; beast; Beyoncé; big bag; big H; big Harry; bird; birdie powder; *birria*; *birria blanca*; black; black bitch; black goat; black olives; black paint; black pearl; black sheep; black shirt; black tar; *blanco*; blue; blow dope; blue hero; *bombita* (heroin mixed with **cocaine**); bombs away; *bonita*; boy; bozo; *brea negra*; brick gum; brown; brown crystal; brown rhine; brown sugar; bubble gum; burrito; butter; *caballo*; *caballo negro*; *caca*; café; *cajeta*; capital H; cardio (white heroin); *carga*; caro; cement; *certificada* (pure heroin); *chapopote*; charlie; charlie horse; *chavo*; cheese; *chicle*; *chiclosa*; China; *China blanca* (white heroin); China cat; China white; Chinese buffet (white heroin); Chinese food; Chinese red; chip; *chiva*; *chiva blanca*; *chiva loca* (heroin mixed with **fentanyl**); *chiva negra*; *chivones*; chocolate; chocolate balls; chocolate shake; choko; *chorizo*; *churro negro*; *chutazo*; coco; coffee; *cohete*; *comida*; crown crap; curly hair; dark; dark girl; dark kind; dead on arrival (DOA); diesel; dirt; dog food; doggie; doojee; dope; dorado; down; downtown; dragon; dreck; dynamite; dyno; *el diablo*; engines; *Enrique Grande*; *esquina*; *esquinilla*; fairy dust; flea powder; food (white heroin); foolish powder; galloping horse; gamot; gato; george smack; girl; globo (balloon of heroin); goat; golden girl; good and plenty; good H; goofball (heroin mixed with **methamphetamine**); *goma*; *gorda*; *gras*; *grasin*; gravy; gum; H; H-caps; hairy; hard candy; hard one; Harry; hats; hazel; heaven dust; heavy; Helen; helicopter; hell dust; Henry; Hercules; hero; him; *hombre*; horse; hot dope; *huera*; hummers; jojee; joy flakes; joy powder; junk; *kabayo*; Karachi; karate; king's tickets; *la tierra*; lemonade; *lenta*; lifesaver; *manteca*; *marias*; Marrion; mayo; mazpan; meal; menthol; Mexican brown; Mexican food (black tar heroin);

Mexican horse; Mexican mud; Mexican treat; *modelo negra*; mojo; mole; *mongega*; *morena*; *morenita*; mortal combat; motors; mud; *mujer*; *murcielago*; muzzle; nanoo; *negra*; *negra tomasa*; *negrita*; nice and easy; night; noise; Obama; old Steve; pants; patty; peg; P-funk; *piezas*; *plata*; poison; *polvo*; *polvo de alegria*; *polvo de estrellas*; *polvo feliz*; poppy; powder; *prostituta negra*; puppy; pure; Rambo; raw (uncut heroin); red chicken; red eagle; reindeer dust; roofing tar; ruby; sack; salt; sand; scag; scat; schmeck; scramble (uncut heroin); sheep; shirts; shoes; skag; skunk; slime; smack; smeck; snickers; soda; speedball (heroin mixed with cocaine); spider blue; sticky kind; *stufa*; sugar; sweet Jesus; tan; tar; *tecata*; thunder; tires; *tomasa*; tootsie roll; tragic magic; trees; turtle; *vidrio*; weights; whiskey; white; white boy; white girl; white junk; white lady; white nurse; white shirt; white stuff; wings; witch; witch hazel; *zapapote*.

H

HH
Half hour (UK police acronym).

highpad
Thief or footpad who robbed on the highway (UK thieves' **cant**, historical slang).

high roller
Gangster or **drug dealer** making a lot of money (US contemporary gang slang).

high-security prison
This is a prison in the UK that houses prisoners who have been given a Category A or B security category because of their risk factors. Currently in the UK there are eight high-security prisons which are: Belmarsh, Frankland, Full

Sutton, Long Lartin, Manchester, Wakefield, Whitemoor and Woodhill.

high-tober

Elite thieves who were always well-dressed and possessed the finest horses. They kept the best company and only robbed on the high road (UK thieves' **cant**, historical slang).

HOCR

See **Home Office Counting Rules**.

hoister

Shoplifter who would go into shops and pretend to buy something while palming other items and hiding them up their sleeves, most often jewellery. A hoister mots was a woman who went into shops and stole small items (UK thieves' **cant**, historical slang).

holding down

Controlling gang turf or an area (US contemporary gang slang).

hollow-point bullet

Bullet with a cavity in the nose to facilitate expansion on impact.

HOLMES 2

See **Home Office Large Major Enquiry System**.

Home Office Counting Rules (HOCR)

The Home Office Counting Rules for recorded crime in the UK stipulate what type and how many offences in any particular incident should be recorded by police and notified to the Home Office.

Home Office Large Major Enquiry System (HOLMES 2)

Computer system used by UK police forces predominantly to aid the **investigation** of large and major incidents such as serial killings and high value, complex **frauds**.

home detention curfew (HDC)

The home detention curfew is commonly known as electronic tagging or electronic monitoring (EM). HDCs allow prisoners to be released from prison before the end of their **sentence** to serve the rest of that sentence with an electronic monitoring device or tag. Prisoners serving a sentence of between three months and four years can be considered for such release. Early release is usually between two weeks and four and half months before the automatic release date, depending on the length of the sentence. An HDC is considered a privilege and not an absolute right of a prisoner. Not all prisoners, such as those who have committed violent or sex crimes, are eligible. When a prisoner is released on an HDC they are required to stay at a designated address and the electronic tag, which resembles a bulky watch, is fitted to them. The tag is waterproof so they can wear it to bathe. It communicates with a monitoring box fitted at their designated address so if they leave it during their curfew hours, normally 7 a.m. to 7 p.m., the control centre will be notified, and the prisoner will be in breach of their HDC. They will then normally be returned to prison to serve the rest of their sentence until their automatic release date.

homeboy, homie

Friend from your own area or neighbourhood; also fellow gang member (UK/US contemporary slang).

honey trap

An operation conducted by an **intelligence agent** or **agency**, private detective or other party who intends to gain information by ensnaring an unwary target in a compromising sexual encounter or a relationship, whether real or merely promised. The target may then be vulnerable to blackmail that could lead to them **spying** or conducting other activities for the person or people who set the trap. Private investigators are often asked to set a honey trap or honey pot to catch a spouse who is suspected of cheating. Honey traps are commonly believed to be set by attractive women but in reality can be laid by members of either sex and used to ensnare someone of either gender.

hot pursuit

Hot pursuit is a US **law enforcement** term. If a criminal flees the scene of a crime and a police officer follows them, the officer has the right in 'hot pursuit' to enter a property in which the criminal has sought shelter.

howdunnit

In contrast to the **whodunnit**, the howdunnit focuses on how a crime, usually a murder, was committed. These stories generally start with the crime having been committed and with the villain already exposed. They then work backwards to expose the truth behind the crime and the **motive** for it.

hue and cry

Before the establishment of police forces in the UK, hue and cry was the method by which criminals were apprehended. It relied on volunteer citizens and involved gathering together bystanders to assist in the apprehension of a person who had been witnessed committing a crime.

human intelligence (humint)

Intelligence derived from information collected and provided by human **sources** and often considered the primary or most valuable source of intelligence for agencies such as **MI6**. There are two basic types of humint – overt and **clandestine**. Overt humint involves meeting a target openly, usually as a diplomatic or military representative of a foreign government, and can include methods such as **interrogation** and observation, while clandestine humint involves intelligence gathering using secret or clandestine means, also known as **espionage**.

human trafficking

Human trafficking is a form of modern slavery and is the illegal harbouring, trade or transport of people through the use of deception and **coercion** for the purposes of exploitation. Victims can be sexually exploited or forced to work, beg or commit criminal acts against their will. They can also have their organs removed and be forced into marriage or domestic servitude. Human trafficking is highly profitable for the organised gangs and criminals who are largely responsible for it. People do not have to be taken across borders in order for trafficking to have occurred and children can be considered trafficked simply if they are taken into an exploitative situation without the need for coercion. Victims of trafficking are often trying to escape extreme poverty, war, violence or lack of opportunity in their country or region. They are often tricked into applying for a job that does not actually exist or where the conditions are completely different to those that were described. They are kept in that situation by violence, force, intimidation, threats against their families and by the removal of their documents as well as the imposition of false debts to their traffickers which they can never pay off.

hush money

Money given to keep someone quiet, especially about a crime or **felony** (UK thieves' **cant**, historical slang and contemporary usage).

hybrid threat

A hybrid threat is the combination of tactics, technologies and capabilities used by adversaries or enemies to gain an asymmetric advantage or edge. These adversaries can include lone attackers, criminals, terrorist organisations and even nation states.

I

IAFIS
See **Integrated Automated Fingerprint Identification System**.

IC
See **Intelligence Community**

ICE
See **Immigration and Customs Enforcement**.

ICP
See **initial contact point**.

IEPs
See **incentives and earned privileges**.

IIO
See **illegal intelligence officer**.

illegal
When used in an **intelligence** context, an illegal is an officer, employee or **agent** of an intelligence organisation who is sent abroad but has no overt relationship with the intelligence service or government for which that person actually works. To all intents and purposes, they are operating as a private person and often under a false identity. This means that they are not afforded diplomatic protection and

can be imprisoned or even executed if caught. They are called illegals because they are operating illegally in the host country. ▶ **illegal intelligence officer (IIO)** Intelligence officer who enters a country with false documents or otherwise circumvents border controls. This means they can stay in that country for an extended period, especially with false documents that allow them to pass background checks and to then leave the country similarly undetected. ▶ **illegal support officer** Intelligence officer who has legal residency in a country and whose primary function is to support illegal **agents** by supplying anything they need. They can also gather information and documents that may be useful to future illegal agents.

illegal drug

Drug that is forbidden by law to possess, use, buy or sell.

imitation firearm

Functional reproduction of an existing **firearm**. The term can also refer to a modern reproduction of an **antique firearm**. Used in crime to fool a victim into believing the weapon is real and to therefore intimidate or terrify them into complying.

Immigration and Customs Enforcement (ICE)

The principal investigative arm of the US Department of Homeland Security (DHS). ICE's primary mission is to promote homeland security and public safety through the criminal and civil enforcement of federal laws governing border control, customs, trade and immigration.

impact spatter

This type of **bloodstain** occurs when blood hits a surface hard and breaks into smaller droplets. The more forceful the impact, the smaller the droplets, with their density decreasing as they move further from the source of the blood. Analysis of impact spatter can help to ascertain the relative positions of individuals and objects at a **crime scene** as well as giving insight into what happened.

impersonal communication

In **intelligence** circles, communications between a **handler** and **asset** that do not involve direct contact. Also, secret communication techniques used between a **case officer** and a **human intelligence** asset when physical contact is not possible or desired.

impressed print

Impressed prints are found in soft materials or tissue at **crime scenes** and are formed by fingers, palms, feet or other body parts pressing into them. They are usually photographed for **evidence** and moulds or **casts** can be made of them.

incentives and earned privileges (IEPs)

Incentives and earned privileges or IEPs are what prisoners in the UK can earn if they follow the rules and take a constructive part in activities, including their **sentence** plan. These incentives and privileges can include things such as more visits from family and friends, more time outside their **cell**, the right to wear their own clothes instead of a prison uniform, the ability to earn and spend more money, and a TV in their cell. IEPs may be taken away if a prisoner behaves badly or does not comply with the rules. There are three IEP levels:

- Basic level: restricted to a prisoner's legal rights such as some letters and visits. Nothing extra is permitted.
- Standard level: a prisoner may be allowed more visits and letters, and possibly a TV in their cell as well as the ability to spend more of their money.
- Enhanced level: a prisoner is allowed even more extras such as more visits, a TV in their cell, or the right to spend more of their money.

inconclusive

Not conclusive; not resolving doubts or questions; without final results or outcome. Can be used of **evidence** and, in **forensic DNA** analysis, can also mean that there is not enough information to include or exclude a person, or that the sample is not suitable for statistics.

Independent Office for Police Conduct (IOPC)

The IOPC is the official public body in the UK that investigates serious **complaints** and **allegations** of misconduct against the police. It replaced the Independent Police Complaints Commission (IPCC) in 2018.

indeterminate sentence for public protection

The indeterminate **sentence** for public protection, sometimes referred to as imprisonment for public protection (IPP), was introduced in the UK in 2005 and abolished in 2012. IPPs allowed judges to set a minimum term to be served but no maximum term and were abolished after it was realised that they were being used too extensively, with nearly 7 per cent of the prison population serving IPPs at one point. Thousands of prisoners on IPPs, who were initially given them for relatively minor crimes in proportion to the sentence, remain in prison unsure of when or if they will be released.

indictable offence

An indictable offence is one that can only be heard on indictment after there has been a preliminary hearing in a Magistrates' Court to decide whether there is a prima facie case to answer. Prima facie is a Latin term that can be loosely translated here as 'at first sight' or 'on the face of it'. The preliminary hearing determines whether there is sufficient corroborating **evidence** to support the fact that there is a case to answer. If it is determined that there is a case to answer for an indictable-only offence then it will be heard in a higher court such as a Crown Court in England and Wales or the High Court or District Court in New Zealand. Examples of indictable offences include **rape** and murder. Indictable offences exist within the common law jurisdictions of England, Scotland and Wales, Ireland, Canada, Australia, the US, Hong Kong, India, New Zealand, Malaysia and Singapore. In the US, an indictable offence is known as a **felony**. A youth court in England and Wales will normally hear all indictable offences apart from homicide and some **firearms** offences provided that its sentencing power of two years' detention is adequate to reflect the seriousness of the crime.

I

infiltration

Placing an **intelligence officer** or **agent** or other person in a target area in hostile territory. Infiltration methods can be **black** or **clandestine**, grey or through a legal crossing point but under false documentation, and white or legal.

informant

Person who knowingly or unknowingly provides information to an **agent**, a **clandestine** or **intelligence** service, or the police.

informer

Someone who intentionally discloses or provides information about other people or activities to police or a **security service**, usually for a financial reward.

infraction

An infraction (sometimes called a violation) is a petty offence in the US that is punishable only by a small fine. Because infractions cannot result in a jail **sentence** or even **probation**, defendants **charged** with infractions do not have a right to a jury trial.

initial contact point (ICP)

The physical location where an **intelligence officer** or **agent** makes an initial contact or **brush contact** with his **source** or **asset**.

injunction

Court **order** to stop doing or to start doing a specific act.

insect bloodstain

As its name suggests, this is caused by an insect, especially a type of fly that likes to feed on blood and tissue, at the scene. The blood is then regurgitated by the fly as a small, circular stains known as flyspeck. Insects can also move through **bloodstains**, causing further, smaller stains and patterns.

Integrated Automated Fingerprint Identification System (IAFIS)

The **Federal Bureau of Investigation**'s automated **fingerprint** system. It is being replaced by the **Next Generation Identification** system.

Intelink

Intelink is the **classified**, worldwide intranet for the US **Intelligence Community**. The most secure level, Intelink-TS, uses the Joint Worldwide Intelligence Communications System (JWICS) to communicate. JWICS is a 24/7 network that is designed to communicate multimedia **intelligence** worldwide up to the Top Secret/Sensitive Compartmented Information level. Intelink-S is a version accessed through the Secret Internet Protocol Router Network (SIPRNet), and accessed at Secret level and above.

intelligence

Intelligence (intel) is often mistakenly assumed simply to mean information when it is far more complex than that, encompassing both the products of information gathering, processing, evaluation, analysis and interpretation as well as the process that leads to the gathering of that information and the organisations and agencies involved in that process. To be useful, intelligence must inform policy or decision makers in such a way that it can be acted upon.

▶**intelligence analyst** Professional intelligence officer who is responsible for performing, coordinating or supervising the collection, analysis and **dissemination** of intelligence. ▶**Intelligence Community (IC)** All the departments or agencies of a government that are concerned with **intelligence** activity. ▶**intelligence officer (IO)** Professionally trained member of an **intelligence** service. He or she may be serving in their home country or abroad, either legally or illegally.

INTERPOL

The International Criminal Police Organization or INTERPOL is the world's largest international police organisation, with 194 member countries. Created in 1923, it is headquartered in Lyon in France and facilitates cross-border police cooperation, supporting and assisting **law enforcement** worldwide.

interrogation

Systematic process of using techniques to question a captured or detained person to obtain reliable information.

investigation

Detailed, systematic, structured and objective inquiry to ascertain the truth about an event, situation or individual, especially after an **allegation** of unlawful or questionable activities. During an investigation, **evidence** is gathered to substantiate or refute the allegation or questionable activity. An investigation is initiated when there are facts or allegations that indicate a possible violation of law or policy.

IO

See **intelligence officer**.

IOPC

See **Independent Office for Police Conduct**.

IPP

See **indeterminate sentence for public protection**.

Irish noir

Genre of crime fiction written by Irish writers and largely set in Ireland although the works of John Connolly, one of its exponents, are set in the United States. Irish noir is characteristically bleak, dark and grim in its realism leavened by moments of gallows humour. It can be further subdivided into genres such as Dublin noir, Ulster noir and Belfast noir.

I

J

jack
Robbery; 'doing a jack' is committing a robbery (US contemporary gang slang).

jacket
Prison inmate's rap sheet or information file; also his reputation among other prisoners (US contemporary slang). See also **bullet jacket**.

Jack-in-the-Box (JIB or jib)
A collapsible or inflatable dummy that is placed in a car to evade **surveillance** or deceive anyone watching about the number of people in the vehicle. Often the jib is in an empty car while the real occupant(s) are elsewhere carrying out **clandestine** or **covert** activities.

jackrabbit parole
To escape from a prison or correctional facility (US contemporary slang).

Jack the Ripper
Perhaps the most infamous serial killer of all, Jack the Ripper was an unknown murderer who stalked the streets of Whitechapel in the East End of London around 1888, killing and mutilating women, mainly

prostitutes. The murders attributed to the person known as Jack the Ripper form only part of what are known as the Whitechapel Murders. The **case file** on these covers eleven cases, five of which are almost certainly attributable to Jack the Ripper, the rest being debatable or definitely not linked to him.

The five believed victims of Jack the Ripper, often referred to as the canonical five victims, are Mary Ann Nichols, Annie Chapman, Elizabeth Stride, Catherine Eddowes and Mary Kelly, all murdered between August and November 1888, and each of whom had their throat slit and their belly slashed open before being disembowelled. Martha Tabram, also known as Martha Turner, was killed before Mary Ann Nichols and may in fact have been Jack the Ripper's first victim as her throat and abdomen were slashed, although she was not disembowelled. An experienced East End policeman, Inspector Frederick George Abberline, was brought in to head up the **investigation** into the Whitechapel Murders. Wild theories abounded but at least the increased police presence in the area appeared to have scared off the murderer until the night of 30 September 1888 when he killed two more victims, Elizabeth Stride and then Catherine Eddowes, little more than an hour apart.

The killer acquired his name from a letter that was sent to a London news agency, written in red ink and boasting of what the killer had done as well as what he planned to do. The letter was signed Jack the Ripper. Although the police quickly deduced the letter was a hoax and actually written by a journalist, they had already publicised it and unleashed a deluge of other letters, some clearly hoaxes too and others more questionable. In November 1888, the body of the woman believed to be the Ripper's final victim, Mary Kelly, was found in her room in Whitechapel, skinned almost to the bone.

There were several more Whitechapel Murders believed to have been the work of different perpetrators, but it is the Ripper murders that have caught and maintained the public's fascination, throwing up a host of possible suspects, some more plausible than others. To this day, the crimes remain unsolved and are likely to remain that way. The Ripper murders not only gave rise to rudimentary criminal **profiling** but were also the first to attract a worldwide media frenzy. They have also inspired hundreds of fiction and non-fiction books, songs, plays, operas, films and TV series, including a film for Japanese TV featuring your author as Catherine Eddowes.

jam

Jam or jam roll means **parole** (UK cockney rhyming and contemporary prison slang).

jammer

Knife, usually homemade (UK contemporary prison slang).

Jane/John Doe

Jane Doe and John Doe are standard placeholder names used by **law enforcement** and the courts when a corpse or living person is unidentified, fictitious or must remain anonymous. **Richard Roe** or the surname Roe are also used in court cases when two parties must remain anonymous, most famously in the US Supreme Court case of *Roe vs Wade*. The surnames Doe and Roe come from an antiquated British legal property process and, interestingly, both reference deer.

jaunt

Derived from joint and can refer to anything from a weapon such as a **shank** to prison currency such as a **magazine** or book of stamps. Used between prisoners so cops and guards won't know what they are talking about (US contemporary prison slang).

Jenny

Lockpick (UK thieves' **cant**, historical slang).

JIB or jib

See **Jack-in-the-Box**

job

Police officers in the UK refer to their profession as 'the job' and may say, 'I'm job' or 'he's in the job' (UK contemporary police slang).

jock-gagger

Man who lives off immoral earnings, usually those of his prostitute wife (UK thieves' **cant**, historical slang).

jointed

Dismembered or beheaded (US/Jamaican contemporary gang slang).

joint intelligence

Intelligence produced by elements or operatives of more than one intelligence service that belong to the same nation.

joint investigation

Investigation in which more than one investigative **agency** has established investigative authority and the agencies involved agree to pursue the investigation on a joint basis having agreed investigative responsibilities, procedures and methods.

jolly

Fake fight staged in the street to act as a distraction while the onlookers are robbed (UK historical slang).

jolt

'Doing a jolt' means doing time in prison (US historical slang).

juke

Hold up, rob or rip someone off (US/Jamaican contemporary gang slang). Also to hit, beat up, poke or stab someone (UK/US slang).

just say no

Alert that **undercover** police are in the area (US contemporary gang slang).

K

K

To kill. If someone adds a k to the end of their name it means they have killed at least one person (London contemporary gang slang associated with drill music). Also slang for **ketamine**.

kanga

Prison officer, from kangaroo which, in cockney rhyming slang, rhymes with **screw**, another term for a prison officer (UK contemporary prison slang).

Kate

Lockpick (UK thieves' **cant**, historical slang).

keister

To hide something such as **drugs** in the anal cavity (US contemporary prison slang).

ketamine

Ketamine (ketamine hydrochloride) is a dissociative anaesthetic and analgesic that is frequently used as a **date-rape drug** because it paralyses its victim for at least a brief period of time. Its dissociative effects are so powerful they can cause auditory and visual hallucinations. When mixed with other depressant drugs and **alcohol**, ketamine's depressant effect on the airways can be deadly. There is also a risk that the temporary paralysis it induces can cause a victim to be unable to clear their airways, thereby choking to death. Ketamine can be detected in urine up to three to five days after ingestion. Street names include: Barry Farrell; blind squid; cat food; cat Valium; donkey; green; green K; honey oil; jet; jet K; K; keller; Kelly's day; K-hold; kit kat; kitty flip; K-ways; purple; Special K; special la coke; super acid; super C; vitamin K; wobble; wonky.

keylogger

Non-destructive program that is designed to log every keystroke made on a computer. The information that is collected can then be saved as a file and/or sent to another computer on the network or over the internet, making it possible for someone else to see every keystroke that was made on a particular system. Using this information, a **cracker** can recreate your usernames and passwords, putting all kinds of data and information at risk. Some companies install keyloggers on employee computers to track usage and ensure that systems are not being used for unintended purposes. Keyloggers are, for obvious reasons, often considered to be **spyware**.

kick up

US **Mafia** term for passing the proceeds of criminal activity up the chain of command.

kidnapper

Historically, a kid-napper is someone who abducts children; also a decoy for street robberies (UK thieves' **cant**, historical slang). The word 'kidd' for a child was also thieves' **cant** or historical slang. The contemporary word kidnapper is a direct contraction of the original usage and now means someone who abducts a person of any age.

kifer

Implement used by burglar (UK Victorian slang).

kill

To cause the death of or end of the life of a person, animal or plant. In crime fiction, especially **hard-boiled**, detective and gangster fiction, there are numerous terms for 'to kill' including: annihilate; assassinate; blip off; blow; bop; bump; bump off; burn; chill off; croak; cut down; decimate; do for; do away with; do in; eradicate; erase; euthanise; execute; finish; finish off; get; ice; knock off; liquidate; massacre; murder; **neutralise**; obliterate; off; put away; pop; poop; rub out; scrag; snuff; take out; total; waste; whack; wipe; zap; zotz.

As a noun, a kill can be anything that has been slaughtered, including an animal or a person.

Killing, The

Successful Danish **police procedural** TV series (*Forbrydelsen* [The Crime] in Danish) created by Søren Sveistrup and first broadcast on national TV station DR1 on 7 January 2007. Since then, it has been transmitted worldwide with the US remake first airing in 2011. The original version is set in Copenhagen, and revolves around Detective Inspector Sarah Lund, played by Sofie Gråbøl. It is notable in boosting the popularity of the hugely successful genre known as **Scandi noir**.

kinchin

Young children (UK thieves' **cant**, historical slang). Kinchin coves were men who stole or procured children for gypsies and beggars to be used to elicit sympathy and aid criminal activity (UK thieves' **cant**, historical slang).

kite

Originally a worthless cheque, this now refers to any cheque. To say you were going to 'fly a kite' meant you were going to pass a bad cheque. Also US prison slang for an illicit letter that is passed from **cell** to cell, sometimes shaped like a kite and used for purposes such as placing orders for **drugs**.

▶ **kiter** Someone who writes bad cheques (UK/US slang in popular use in 1980s–90s and still in use today).

knap

To steal or take. Knapped is the past tense means stolen or taken (UK thieves' **cant**, historical slang).

knife crime

Knife crime is defined in the UK as any offence that is classified as homicide, **attempted** murder, **assault** with intent to cause harm, assault with injury, threats to kill, sexual offences (including **rape**) and **robbery** where a knife or sharp instrument has been used to injure, used as a threat, or the victim was convinced a knife was present during the offence. ▶ **knife possession** Knife possession offences are defined in the UK as having an article with blade or point in a public place (including school), threatening with a blade or sharply pointed article in a public place (including school), possession of an offensive weapon, using someone to look after an offensive weapon and threatening with an offensive weapon.

kom ind

Danish for 'come in', often seen in **Scandi noir**.

KSI

Killed or seriously injured (UK police acronym).

L

lag

Someone who has been frequently convicted and sent to prison, often referred to as an 'old lag', a term of unknown origin. ▶ **lagged** Transported to the colonies for a crime (UK Victorian slang).

land shark

Police dog, also known as a 'furry Exocet' or a 'hairy Exocet' (UK police slang).

larceny

Larceny is defined in the US as the unlawful taking, carrying, leading or riding away of property from the possession or constructive possession of another or **attempting** to commit these acts. Larceny includes **shoplifting**, **pickpocketing**, purse-snatching, bicycle **theft** and similar acts in which no use of force, violence or **fraud** occurs.

latent print

One of three categories of **fingerprints** that can be found at a **crime scene**, the others being **impressed** and **patent prints**. A latent print is an impression that is not visible to the naked eye. They are composed of the sweat, skin salts and oils and tiny particles of dirt that we all carry and transfer from our hands even when they appear clean. Latent prints are made visible using magnesium powder, which is dusted over surfaces to illuminate them so they can then be

lifted. They can also be revealed through the use of chemicals including cyanoacrylate (found in superglue) and silver nitrate.

late turn
Police shift or tour of duty that starts at 2 p.m. (UK police slang).

law enforcement
Generic term for the activities of agencies responsible for maintaining public order and enforcing the law. These include the prevention, detection and **investigation** of crime, and the apprehension of criminals to protect people, places and things from criminal activity.

lawful search
Examination, authorised by law, of a specific person, property or area to locate specified property **evidence**, or of a specific person for the purpose of seizing such property or evidence.

laws, strange or weird
Many countries have strange or obscure laws that are often left over from archaic legislation although some are surprisingly modern. In the UK, some examples include:

- All beached whales and sturgeons must be offered to the reigning monarch.
- It is illegal to be drunk in a pub.
- MPs are not allowed to wear armour in parliament.

- It is an offence to be drunk and in charge of cattle in England and Wales.
- It is illegal to handle a salmon in suspicious circumstances.

In the US, some state laws are equally bizarre:

- In Idaho cannibalism is strictly prohibited and punishable by up to fourteen years in prison, except under 'life-threatening conditions as the only apparent means of survival'.
- In Kentucky every legislator, public officer and lawyer must take an oath stating that they have not fought a duel with **deadly weapons**.
- In Maryland anyone 'pretending to forecast or foretell the future of another by cards, palm-reading or any other scheme, practice or device' can be found guilty of a **misdemeanour** and fined up to $500, or even serve time in jail.
- In Tennessee it is a Class A misdemeanour to deliberately hunt, trap or harm an albino deer.

Strange laws are not confined to the UK and US. In Mexico you may not lift your feet from the pedals if you are riding a bicycle; in Switzerland it is forbidden to hike while naked; and you are not permitted to urinate in the sea in Portugal, although how they police that last one is anyone's guess.

lay

Job. **Hard-boiled** fiction term, as used by Phillip Marlowe in *The Big Sleep* (1939) when he's describing a private detective on a confidential job: 'Private – on a confidential lay.' Also used to describe a situation: 'I gave him the lay', i.e. 'I told him where things stood' (as in 'lie of the land').

lead

Source or potential source of information that may provide a clue or **evidence** in the **investigation** of a crime. Also, in **intelligence** usage, a person with potential for exploitation or any source of information that, if exploited, may reveal information of value in the conduct of an intelligence operation or investigation.

lead bullet

Compact **bullet** formed by a lead alloy.

legal thriller

See **courtroom drama**.

legend

See **cover legend**.

leng

Weapon or gun (UK/US contemporary slang).

lethal

Certain to or intended to cause death. Can be used of force, weapons, intent or quantity, especially where **drugs** are concerned.

lid

Police hat or helmet (UK police slang).

lift

A lift is the adhesive tape or another medium used when **fingerprints** need to be lifted, or recovered, and preserved from a **crime scene** or from **evidence**. Electrostatic, gelatine and adhesive lifts are all common methods.

light weapon

Light weapons, according to NATO definitions, are collective **firearms** designed to be used by two or three persons, though some of them can be used single-handedly.

listening post

Secure site at which signals from an audio operation are received and/or monitored.

Little, Samuel

Samuel Little (b. 1940) has been confirmed by the **Federal Bureau of Investigation** as the most prolific serial killer in American history. He has confessed to ninety-three murders with at least fifty of those having been confirmed so far by **law enforcement**. Little claims to have strangled his victims between 1970 and 2005, although many of those deaths were initially attributed to overdoses or natural causes. The FBI's **Violent Criminal Apprehension Program** (ViCAP) began to link Little, who was already serving three life **sentences** without **parole**, to these crimes in 2014. He had initially been **arrested** in 2012 on **drugs charges** in California and **DNA** then taken while he was in **custody** linked him to three unsolved homicides in the 1980s. A Texas Ranger went to interview the septuagenarian in 2017 and Little confessed to killing his victims – who were mostly prostitutes or otherwise living on the fringes of society – on camera from behind bars. He drew portraits of thirty of them, many of them African American like himself, and described others as well as how he had killed each one. He has already pleaded guilty to murdering four women in Ohio and the FBI have provided information about five more homicides in Florida, Arkansas, Kentucky, Nevada and Louisiana, asking the public for help in identifying the victims. Authorities in Knoxville, Tennessee, have said that a woman named Martha Cunningham, whose body was found in 1975, is also likely to be a victim of Little. Little thought he would never be caught for his crimes because no one was accounting for his victims, but the FBI is now determined to identify each one to bring closure to their families and loved ones.

L

load
Combination of components used to assemble a gun **cartridge**. Load also refers to the act of putting **ammunition** into the **chamber** of a **firearm**.

local nick
Term for local police station used by the police and criminals (UK contemporary slang).

locked-room mystery
The locked-room mystery, a subgenre of detective fiction, involves a **crime scene** in which it is apparently impossibly for a perpetrator to get into and out of undetected, i.e. a 'locked room'. Typically, the crime is a murder and the perpetrator appears to have vanished into thin air. As with classic detective fiction, the reader is presented with the mystery to be solved along with the clues so they can attempt to deduce what has happened along with the detective or investigator.

lividity

Lividity, also known as livor mortis or postmortem hypostatis, is the process by which blood stops flowing around the body when the heart stops pumping after death. The blood normally responds to gravity, which means that someone found lying on their back will have all the blood from their front draining towards the ground. Lividity results in dark purple discolouration of the body, and any part of the body that has been in prolonged contact with a hard surface such as the floor will display signs of it. Lividity starts to work through the body within half an hour of the heart stopping and can continue for up to twelve hours. For the first six hours after it has begun, it can be disturbed by any movement of the body but after that point the blood vessels begin to break down and it cannot be altered. This means that lividity is also used as a reliable indicator of time of death.

L

Locard's Exchange Principle

Dr Edmond Locard (1877–1966), 'the Sherlock Holmes of France', was a French criminologist and pioneer of **forensic** science who came up with a theory that can be summarised as 'every contact leaves a trace'. He believed that a perpetrator takes something into a **crime scene** and also takes something from it whether that be hair, clothing fibres, blood traces or **fingerprints**. Both can be used as **forensic evidence**. This became known as Locard's Exchange Principle and is the foundation of all forensic science today.

lock-down

Locking **cells** either at set times or as a response to a
particular situation (UK contemporary prison slang).

logic bomb

Malicious program designed to execute when a certain
criterion is met. A logic bomb can be designed to execute
when a particular file is accessed, or when a certain key
combination is pressed, or through the actioning of any
other event or task that is possible to be tracked on a
computer. The logic bomb remains dormant until the trigger event occurs.

LOS

Lost or stolen (UK police acronym).

LSD

See **Lysergic Acid Diethylamide**.

lully-prigger

Lowest and meanest order of thieves who lured little children to dark alleyways and blindspots where they robbed
them of their clothes (UK thieves' **cant**, historical slang).

luminol

Luminol ($C_8H_7O_3N_2$) is a powder compound composed of
carbon, hydrogen, oxygen and nitrogen. It is mixed with
hydrogen peroxide and an alkali such as sodium hydroxide
to create the liquid that is sprayed at **crime scenes** to
detect traces of blood. It does so by luminescing in the presence of blood, emitting its characteristic blue glow that is
bright enough to see in a dark room. This is caused by a
reaction between the hydrogen peroxide and luminol

accelerated by the iron contained in haemoglobin. The same reaction can occur in the presence of other substances including faeces and bleach.

lysergic acid diethylamide (LSD)

LSD, also known as 'acid', is a powerful **hallucinogenic drug** that is usually sold as small squares of paper, known as tabs or blotters, with pictures on, or in liquid form or as micro dots known as pellets. While the liquid form has no taste, the paper form tastes of paper. LSD **trips** can last for hours and cause disturbing hallucinations as well as euphoria, excitement, paranoia or aggression, depending on the person's state of mind when they take the drug. LSD is not **addictive**, although prolonged use requires increased dosage. It is a Class A drug and carries a maximum seven-year prison **sentence** for possession in the UK. LSD's street names include: aceite; acelide; acid; acido; Alice; angels in the sky; animal; Avandaro; backbreaker (LSD mixed with **strychnine**); barrel; Bart Simpson; battery acid; beast; big D; black acid (LSD mixed with **PCP**); black star; black sunshine; black tabs; *blanco de España*; blotter acid; blotter cube; blue acid; blue barrel; blue chair; blue cheer; blue heaven; blue microdots; blue mist; blue moon; blue sky; blue star; blue tabs; *bomba*; brown bomber; brown dots; California sunshine; cherry dome; chief; Chinese dragons; *Cid*; coffee; *colorines*; conductor; contact lens; crackers; crystal tea; cubo; cupcakes; dental floss; dinosaurs; *divina*; domes; dots; double dome; *El Cid*; electric Kool Aid; *elefante blanco*; Ellis Day; fields; flash; flat blues; ghost; golden dragon; golf

L

balls; goofy; gota; grape parfait; green wedge; grey shields; hats; Hawaiian sunshine; hawk; haze; headlights; heavenly blue; hits; instant zen; Jesus Christ acid; kaleidoscope; Leary; lens; *lentejuela*; lime acid; live, spit and die; *lluvia de estrellas*; Looney Tunes; Lucy; *maje*; mellow yellow; mica; microdot; *micropunto azul* (white tablet with drop of blue LSD); *micropunto morado* (white tablet with drop of purple LSD); Mighty Quinn; mind detergent; Mother of God; *mureler*; nave; newspapers; orange barrels; orange cubes; orange haze; orange micros; orange wedges; owsley; paper acid; pearly gates; pellets; phoenix; pink blotters; Pink Panther; pink robots; pink wedges; pink witches; pizza; pop; potato; pure love; purple barrels; purple haze; purple hearts; purple flats; recycle; royal blues; Russian sickles; sacrament; *sandoz*; smears; square dancing tickets; sugar cubes; sugar lumps; sunshine; superman; tabs; *tacatosa*; tail lights; teddy bears; ticket; Uncle Sid; valley dolls; vodka acid; wedding bells; wedge; white dust; white fluff; white lightening; white owsley; window glass; window pane; yellow dimples; yellow sunshine; zen.

M

MacDonald Triad

This is the name given to the three classic behaviours which, if exhibited in childhood, were claimed to be a predictor of violent tendencies in later life. These behaviours are excessive bed-wetting beyond the age of five, cruelty to animals and fire-starting, and the phrase was coined in a 1963 paper entitled 'The Threat to Kill' published in *The American Manual of Psychiatry* by J. M. MacDonald. MacDonald's research group was small and unrepresentative, as were subsequent, badly designed groups which bore out his results. When tested in larger groups with better controls, his results could not be replicated. The MacDonald Triad cannot therefore be considered a reliable predictor of future murderers or serial killers despite the reliance on it by some authors and even criminologists.

machine
Machine gun (US/Jamaican contemporary gang slang).

machine gun
Also known as a fully **automatic firearm**. A weapon that fires rapidly and repeatedly without requiring separate pressure on the **trigger** each time The gun will continue to fire until the trigger is released or the supply of

ammunition is exhausted. ▶ **machine pistol** Fully **automatic handgun** such as the **Glock 18**. The term machine pistol can also be used to refer to a **sub-machine gun**.

made man

Someone who has been inducted into the US **Mafia**.

Mafia

The term Mafia originated with the Sicilian **organised crime** families who formed a loose syndicate although they do not use the word, preferring to refer to themselves as *Cosa Nostra*, meaning 'our thing'. Through generations of emigration, the Sicilian Mafia spread to the US and Canada, carrying out their traditional activities of protection racketeering or the provision of security services to businesses in exchange for payment and under threat of violence. Smuggling, loan sharking, vote rigging and murder are other traditional Sicilian Mafia activities, which have been adopted by other organised crime syndicates who emulate the original gangsters. There are now international organisations referred to as Mafias in the media, although they prefer to use their own names such as *Bratva* (Russian), *Yakuza* (Japanese), *La Eme* (Mexican) and *Mutra* (Bulgarian). **Drug trafficking** and prostitution rackets are now major activities for most Mafia organisations.

magazine

Spring-loaded box or tube that holds **cartridges** ready for **loading** into the **chamber** of a repeating or self-loading gun. It may be removable or an integral/fixed part of the **firearm**.

Magnum

Term commonly used to describe a gun **cartridge** that is longer than a standard cartridge or shell of a given **calibre** with an increase over standard performance.

mainlining

Act of injecting an **illegal drug**, especially **heroin** or **cocaine**, into a large vein.

malware

Malicious program that causes damage to a computer or computer system. It includes **viruses**, **Trojans**, **worms**, **time bombs**, **logic bombs** or anything else intended to cause damage upon the execution of the **payload**.

manslaughter

Legal term for homicide that is considered to be less culpable than murder. There are different types of manslaughter including voluntary manslaughter, where the perpetrator intended to kill the victim but acted in the moment and did so in circumstances that would cause a reasonable person to become emotionally or mentally disturbed. This could include defending themselves from a sudden attack or when provoked. Involuntary manslaughter occurs when the perpetrator did not intend to kill the victim. It is further divided into the categories of constructive manslaughter, where the perpetrator kills the victim in the course of committing an unlawful act such as dangerous driving, and criminally negligent manslaughter where death occurs as the result of gross negligence on the part of the perpetrator. Manslaughter referred to in England and Wales as gross negligence manslaughter is called criminally negligent homicide in the US.

marking

Types of marking on a gun include letters, **serial numbers**, words or symbols that are stamped, rolled, cast or engraved on the **firearm** to designate the manufacturer, model, origin, **calibre** or **gauge**, choke (tapered constriction of a gun barrel), material or proof that the gun is safe to be used with its designated ammunition. Important in the identification of a gun, markings are often filed off or otherwise removed by criminals who want a weapon to be untraceable.

martial arts weapon

Martial arts weapons include the nunchaku, kama, kasari-fundo, octagon sai, tonfa and Chinese star.

mash

Handgun. ▶ **mash man** Gunman (London contemporary gang slang associated with drill music).

mask of sanity

The name given to the ability of some psychopaths to blend in thanks to their adoption of a mask of apparently normal behaviour. Despite this apparently normal, intelligent and even charming behaviour, these psychopaths are unable to experience genuine emotions, and this leads to destructive or self-destructive behaviour. It was coined by the psychiatrist Hervey M. Cleckley in his book *The Mask of Sanity: An Attempt to Clarify Some Issues About the So-Called Psychopathic Personality*, first published in 1941 and based on his interviews with patients in a locked institution. Famous criminal examples include **Ted Bundy**, Charles Manson and **John Wayne Gacy**.

master program

In **cybercrime**, a master program is the program a **cracker** uses remotely to transmit commands to infected **zombie drones**, normally to carry out denial of service (DoS) attacks or **spam** attacks.

MCT

See **Missing Children's Team**.

MDMA

MDMA (3,4-methylenedioxy-methamphetamine) was originally developed in 1912 by Merck and used in **psychological warfare** experiments by the US Army in 1953. MDMA in its original form was used to lower inhibitions. It did not become known as a party **drug** until the 1970s and was only made illegal in 1985 due to safety concerns. MDMA is particularly dangerous because the pills now being sold on the street may contain a variety of substances including rat **poison**, **heroin**, **cocaine** and **methamphetamine**, while being composed of little or no actual MDMA. A number of deaths, half of them of teenagers, have resulted from taking adulterated MDMA pills. MDMA is also known as: Adam; baby slits; beans; blue kisses; blue Superman; bomb; booty juice (dissolved in liquid); candy; chocolate chips; clarity; dancing shoes; decadence; disco biscuit; doctor; domex (ecstasy mixed with **PCP**); drop; E; E-bomb; essence; Eve; go; goog; green apple; happy pill; hug; hug drug; Kleenex; love doctor; love drug; love flip (taken with mescaline); Love Potion #9; love trip (ecstasy mixed with mescaline); lover's speed; Malcolm X; moon rock; peace; pingaz; pinger; roll; rolling; running; scooby snacks; skittle; smack; slit; smartie; speed for lovers; sweet; tacha; thizz; vitamin E; vowel; white Mercedes; X; XTC; yoke.

medical examiner (ME)

The medical examiner is a medically trained professional who officially investigates suspicious deaths or those that occur in unusual circumstances. The ME carries out post-mortems and can initiate inquests. In the UK, a medical examiner must have undergone formal medical training and will usually also be trained in pathology. In the US, most jurisdictions require formal medical training and further training in pathology, but some have less stringent requirements. A medical examiner has wide-ranging duties and must be able to rely on extensive **forensic** knowledge.

metabolite

Substance produced by metabolism or that is necessary for the metabolic process. It is what is left after the body breaks down a substance or changes it into another chemical. Most **drugs** metabolise in the body and the metabolites they produce are identified through **forensic toxicology**.

metallic cartridge

Ammunition that has a metallic **cartridge case**.

methamphetamine

Methamphetamine is a stronger form of **amphetamine**. It is highly **addictive** and is the second most popular **illegal drug** globally after **cannabis**. It can be injected, snorted or swallowed and is a powerful **stimulant** but can cause brain damage and psychosis, among other health risks. Smoking the purer crystalline form known as crystal meth results in an intense high similar to that produced by **crack cocaine**, although it lasts longer. Methamphetamine is a Class B drug in the UK unless prepared for injection, when it becomes Class A. It is also commonly called: accordion; amp; aqua; *arroz*; assembled (crystal meth); *batu*; *begok*; biker's coffee; blue; blue bell ice cream; beers; bottles; *bucio*; Bud Light; bump; *cajitas*; chalk; chandelier; *chav-alone*; chicken; chicken feed; chicken powder; Chris; Christine; Christy; clear; clothing cleaner; cold; cold one; Colorado rockies; crank; cream; cri-cri; crink; crisco; Crissy; crypto; crystal; *cuadro*; day; diamond; dunk; *El Gata Diablo*; evil sister; eye glasses; fire; fizz; flowers; *foco*; food; *frio*; fruit; *gak*; garbage; G-funk; gifts; girls; glass; go-fast; go-go; goofball (methamphetamine mixed with **heroin**); groceries; hard ones; hare; Hawaiian salt; hielo; hiropon; hot ice; hubbers; ice; ice cream; ice water; icehead; jale; jug of water; LA glass; LA ice; lemons; lemon drop; light; light beige; *livianas*; *madera*; mamph; meth; methlies quick; Mexican crack; Mexican crank; Miss Girl; *montura*; motor; *muchacha*; nails; one pot; no-doze; paint; *pantalones*; *patudas*; peanut butter crank; *piñata*; pointy ones; *pollito*; popsi-cle; purple; *raspado*; rims; rocket fuel; salt; *shabu*; shards; shatter; shaved ice; shiny girl; small girl; soap dope; soft ones; speed; speed dog; spicy kind; spin; stove top; stuff; super ice; table; tina; tires; trash; truck; Tupperware; tweak; unassembled (powder meth); uppers; *Ventanas*; *vidrio*; walking zombie; water; wazz; white; whizz; windows; witches teeth; yaba; yellow barn; yellow cake; yellow kind; zip.

M

Metropolitan Police Service (MPS)

The Metropolitan Police Service, commonly known as the Metropolitan Police or Met, is the police service responsible for all thirty-two London boroughs that fall within the Metropolitan Police District, apart from the City of London, which is policed by the **City of London Police**. As the police service based in the capital, the Metropolitan Police Service has significant national responsibilities including protecting the royal family, embassies, government buildings and government officers as well as leading **counterterrorism** activities. It is also responsible for protecting Heathrow Airport and is the largest police force in the UK.

misdemeanour

A misdemeanour in the US is a criminal offence punishable by up to a year in jail. Punishment for misdemeanours can also include a fine, **probation**, community service and restitution. Defendants **charged** with misdemeanours are entitled to a jury trial.

MI5

MI5 (Military Intelligence, Section 5) is officially known as the **Security Service** and is the UK's domestic and **counterintelligence** security **agency**. It deals with threats to national security including terrorism, cyber threats and **espionage** while protecting the UK's parliamentary and economic interests. It is also concerned with counter-proliferation against regimes that have developed **weapons of mass destruction** (WMDs) and act in contravention of United Nations resolutions, develop **clandestine** weapons or refuse to sign up to the Non-Proliferation Treaty. MI5 gathers **intelligence**, works in partnership with other national and international agencies, and carries out clandestine and **covert** operations both in the UK and abroad. It is based at Thames House in London and has featured in books, films and TV series, including *Spooks* (2002–11), which was renamed *MI-5* in the US.

MI6

MI6 (Military Intelligence, Section 6) is officially known as the Secret Intelligence Service (SIS) and is the UK government's **foreign intelligence** service. Its role is the **covert** gathering and analysis of **human intelligence** overseas in order to protect the United Kingdom. Since 1995 MI6 has been headquartered at 85 Vauxhall Cross on the Albert Embankment in London, a building famously featured in the James Bond film *The World Is Not Enough* (1999). Bond is, of course, a fictional MI6 operative and the agency has also been featured in numerous books, films and TV series, notably those works of John le Carré, a former SIS **agent**, whose real name is David Cornwell.

M

misper

A misper (short for 'missing person') is a person whose whereabouts cannot be established (UK police slang). In the UK, a missing person will be assessed according to risk and the likelihood of coming to harm on a scale ranging from no apparent risk to high risk, the latter almost always resulting in a rapid **deployment** of police resources.

Missing Children's Team (MCT)

Part of the **National Crime Agency**'s **Child Exploitation and Online Protection Command**. See **Missing Persons Unit**..

Missing Persons Unit (MPU)

The Missing Persons Unit (MPU) and the **Missing Children's Team** are both part of the **National Crime Agency**'s **Child Exploitation and Online Protection Command** in the UK, and work with police and other organisations to improve services to missing people and their families. The MPU serves all UK police forces as well as international and overseas police agencies, and is a part of a wider network that includes other government departments and non-governmental organisations. It holds a database of missing persons, unidentified bodies, remains and people found in the UK, and matches **cases** across police force boundaries.

The MPU also manages the **forensic** databases associated with missing and unidentified **investigations**, undertakes desk-based enquiries on behalf of forces and sends advisers to provide investigative advice and support on a case-by-case basis for both new and **cold-case** investigations. Police forces in the UK must submit case details to the MPU in relation to all people reported missing in the UK who are still missing after seventy-two hours; all foreign nationals reported as missing in the UK via **INTERPOL** or any other means; and all UK residents reported as missing abroad. If a case is of particular concern, perhaps when a serious crime is suspected and/or there is significant public or media interest, then it has to be sent to the MPU immediately. All reports of unidentified bodies or people must be sent to the MPU within forty-eight hours of discovery. This is to assist major crime investigations and to bring closure to the families of missing people who are deceased.

MO

See **modus operandi**.

Mob

Single **Mafia** family or a term referring to all **organised crime** families, or Mafia. ▶ **mobbed up** Connected to the Mob. ▶ **mobster** Someone who is part of the Mafia or belongs to the Mob.

modus operandi (MO)

The modus operandi (Latin for 'way of operating') or MO is the particular way or method in which someone does something. In the context of criminal **investigations** it is the particular method or pattern used by a criminal that indicates their involvement in more than one crime.

mole

Member of an organisation such as the police or **intelligence** service who is **spying** and reporting on their own organisation. The mole may already be working for the intelligence service or other highly **sensitive** organisation when they begin divulging information, or they may be inserted into it for that purpose. Quite often a mole is a potential defector who agrees to spy in return for help defecting. In John le Carré's novel, *Tinker, Tailor, Soldier, Spy* (1974), his protagonist Smiley has to hunt down a mole in **MI6**/Secret Intelligence Service. ▶ **mole hunt** Term popularised by John le Carré for an **investigation** conducted into a suspected mole or hostile penetration.

moll buzzer

Someone who only steals from women (US historical slang).

money laundering

Process used to disguise the origin of what are usually large amounts of money obtained from criminal or illicit activity, and to make it seem as if it has come from a legitimate source. The process can include property purchases, shell companies that appear legitimate but do not have any assets or perform any business activities, and investment schemes. Money laundering helps to finance **organised crime** and terrorist activity, threatening national and international security.

Moors Murders

The Moors Murders was a series of murders that took place in and around Manchester in the United Kingdom between July 1963 and October 1965. The murders were carried out by Ian Brady and Myra Hindley and all the victims were children. Of the five victims, who were aged between ten and seventeen years old, at least four had been sexually **assaulted**. Brady and Hindley were **charged** with the murders of three of the victims. Although they both pleaded not guilty, photographs of the moors where the murders took place were discovered in a suitcase belonging to the couple and displayed in court along with pornographic photographs of one of their victims, Lesley Ann Downey, with a scarf tied across her mouth. A tape recording was also played in court of the torture of Lesley Ann Downey who could be heard begging and screaming for help. Brady and Hindley both received life **sentences**. In 1985, Brady reportedly confessed to two more of the murders and later he and Hindley were taken separately to Saddleworth Moor where two of their other victims had been discovered. After a subsequent visit to the moor by Hindley in 1987, the body of Pauline Reade, their first victim, was discovered a hundred yards from where that of Lesley Ann Downey had been found. Myra Hindley was depicted by the press as the most evil woman in Britain and, despite making several **appeals** against her life sentence, was never released. She died in 2002, aged sixty. Ian Brady was diagnosed as a psychopath in 1985 and stated that he never wished to be released, repeatedly asking to be allowed to die. He died in 2017, aged seventy-nine, and took the whereabouts of the remains of one of his victims, Keith Bennett, to his grave.

mop
Large gun (London contemporary gang slang associated with drill music).

Moscow Rules
Ultimate **tradecraft** methods for use in the most hostile operational environments. During the Cold War, Moscow was considered the most difficult operating environment for a **spy** or **intelligence agent** or operative.

motive
Reason someone commits an offence or crime. Intent is a factor in deciding guilt or innocence and therefore establishing motive can be vital along with the other important factors of means and opportunity.

MPS
See **Metropolitan Police Service**.

MPU
See **Missing Persons Unit**.

Munchausen syndrome by proxy

Mental illness that manifests in a carer or caregiver of a child inventing fictitious symptoms and illnesses affecting that child to seek attention, sometimes harming the child in the process. If the child is harmed this is child abuse and a criminal offence. Sometimes the child is killed, as in the **cases** of Marybeth Tinning of New York, who is suspected of murdering eight of her nine children although she was only convicted of the death of the youngest, for which she was **charged** with second degree murder, and the British nurse Beverley Allitt (see **angel of death**), who killed four of her patients and was charged with harming eleven others.

muppet

Muppet stands for 'Most Useless Police Person Ever Trained' and is considered a term of endearment between officers when engaged in banter. Also a general term for a foolish person.

murder

Murder is considered the most serious form of homicide and occurs when one person unlawfully kills another with the *intention* to cause either death or serious injury. If a person dies through serious harm caused by another, such as though injuries sustained in a premeditated **assault**, where the intention was to cause serious harm or injury, then that is also murder even if the assailant did not actually wish to kill the victim. ▶ **murder weapon** Implement, weapon or object used to commit murder or homicide. The vast majority of homicides in the US are committed with **firearms** while in the UK the most common murder weapon is a knife or other sharp instrument, which is the second most common homicide weapon in the US. The second most common method of killing in the UK is kicking or hitting, and the third strangulation or asphyxiation which, correspondingly, is the third most common method in the US.

musket

Antiquated military matchlock, flintlock or wheel-lock shoulder **firearm** with long **smooth-bore barrel**.

muzzle

Forward end of a gun **barrel** from which the **bullet** or **shot** emerges.

M

N

NABIS
See **National Ballistics Intelligence Service**.

nab the cramp
Be **sentenced** to death (UK thieves' **cant**, historical slang).

NamUs
See **National Missing and Unidentified Persons System**.

narcoterrorism
Terrorism that is linked to illicit **drug trafficking**.

National Ballistics Intelligence Service (NABIS)
NABIS, based in Birmingham, keeps a database of all the guns seized or that otherwise come into police possession in the UK. The service has a **forensic** division that can compare and link **ballistics** to crimes and **cases** in twenty-four to forty-eight hours, an **intelligence cell** that offers intelligence and strategic support to police forces and LEAs (**law enforcement** agencies) and an operational support team. NABIS works with all UK police forces as well as the **National Crime Agency**, British Transport Police, **MI5**, Ministry of Defence Police and the UK Border Force.

National Crime Agency (NCA)

This is the national **law enforcement** organisation in the UK charged with investigating serious and **organised crime**. It is the lead **agency** tackling **money laundering**, **human trafficking**, **drug trafficking**, **cybercrime**, **kidnap** and **extortion**, child sexual abuse and exploitation, illegal **firearms**, **fraud** and economic crime, and border vulnerabilities, although it can investigate any crime. It works across national and international borders, gathering **intelligence**, providing specialist support and capabilities and pursuing the most dangerous criminals, especially those involved in organised crime.

National Crime Information Center (NCIC)

Computerised system of crime records and data, maintained by the **Federal Bureau of Investigation**, that can be accessed by almost every criminal justice **agency** in the United States.

National Crime Recording Standard (NCRS)

This standard was introduced in 2002 after a highly critical review of eight UK police forces' crime-recording procedures found a recording rate that varied between 55 and 82 per cent across the forces. The NCRS aims to be victim-focused and to maintain consistency of recording across all forces. It is based on applying legal definitions of crime to victim's reports.

National Cyber Investigative Joint Task Force (NCIJTF)

The **Federal Bureau of Investigation** is responsible for developing and supporting the NCIJTF, which is the focal point for all US government agencies to coordinate, integrate and share information related to all domestic cyber-threat **investigations**. It includes nineteen **intelligence** and **law enforcement** agencies who work together to identify key players and schemes. It aims to predict and prevent **cyberattacks** as well as pursuing the perpetrators behind them.

National Economic Crime Centre (NECC)

The NECC was established in the UK in 2018 to tackle economic crime including **money laundering**, **fraud**, bribery and corruption. It includes the Joint Money Laundering Intelligence Taskforce.

National Fraud Intelligence Bureau (NFIB)

The National Fraud Intelligence Bureau sits alongside Action Fraud, the national fraud and **cybercrime** reporting centre, within the **City of London Police**, which acts as the national lead for economic crime. The NFIB receives the millions of Action Fraud reports of **fraud** and cybercrime. These are used by the NFIB to identify serial offenders, organised-crime groups and to spot emerging crime types. It does this through assessment and analysis, data matching from different parts of the country and disseminating reports for **investigation**. Bank accounts, websites and phone numbers that are used by fraudsters can be taken down by the NFIB.

National Incident-Based Reporting System (NIBRS)

This is an incident-based reporting system used by **law enforcement** agencies in the United States for collecting and reporting data on crimes. Local, state and federal agencies generate NIBRS data from their records management systems. Data is collected on every incident and **arrest** in the Group A offence category. These Group A offences are forty-six specific crimes grouped in twenty-two offence categories. Specific facts about these offences are gathered and reported in the NIBRS system. In addition to the Group A offences, eleven Group B offences are reported with only the arrest information.

National Integrated Ballistic Information Network (NIBIN)

United States national database of digital images of fired **bullets** and **cartridge cases** from **crime scenes**, operated by the Bureau of Alcohol, Tobacco, Firearms and Explosives (ATF).

National Missing and Unidentified Persons System (NamUs)

In the US, NamUs acts as a clearinghouse for missing, unidentified and unclaimed persons, running a database as well as operating inhouse **forensic** services, including **forensic odontology** and **fingerprint** examination, as well as **forensic anthropology** and **DNA** analyses. It also offers investigative support from experienced professionals. NamUs is funded by the National Institute of Justice and offers all of its services at no cost.

National Police Air Service (NPAS)

The National Police Air Service provides centralised aviation support to all forty-three territorial police forces in England and Wales. Prior to its establishment in 2012, police forces operated their own helicopters.

national security crime

Crime that impacts or is likely to impact on the national security, defence or foreign relations of the United States, including but not limited to **espionage**, sabotage, treason and sedition.

natty lads

Young boy thieves (UK thieves' **cant**, historical slang).

NCA

See **National Crime Agency**.

NCIC

See **National Crime Information Center**.

NCIJTF

See **National Cyber Investigative Joint Task Force**.

NCRS

See **National Crime Recording Standard**.

nerve agent

Potentially **lethal chemical agent** that interferes with the transmission of nerve impulses.

neutralise

To render ineffective or unusable or, particularly when used of people, incapable of interfering with a particular operation. Also to make safe mines, bombs, missiles and booby traps and to render harmless anything contaminated with a **chemical agent**.

Next Generation Identification (NGI)

The **Federal Bureau of Investigation**'s Next Generation Identification biometric database is gradually replacing the current **Integrated Automated Fingerprint Identification System**'s technical capabilities. It is considered the largest biometric database in the world, storing individual **fingerprint** records and other biometric data for criminal and civil matters. Its advanced identification technology provides for fast, efficient and accurate fingerprint processing.

NFA

Initialism for 'No further action', used when someone is released without **charge** or when there will be no further proceedings in a **case**.

NFIB

See **National Fraud Intelligence Bureau**.

NGI

See **Next Generation Identification**.

NIBIN

See **National Integrated Ballistic Information Network**.

NIBRS

See **National Incident-Based Reporting System**.

nick

Police station or prison. Also to **arrest** someone or to steal something (UK contemporary slang).

nickel

Five-year jail **sentence** (US gang slang).

nicker

Prison chaplain, deriving from rhyming slang for vicar (UK contemporary prison slang).

nicotine

Cigarette packets these days often display the warning that 'Smoking Kills'. But nicotine can kill far faster and more directly when used as a **poison**. One particularly famous murder involving the plant alkaloid nicotine took place in Belgium in 1850. The victim was the Belgian aristocrat Gustave Fougnies, who was fed the poison during a family dinner held for him by his sister and brother-in-law, the deeply in debt Comte and Comtesse de Bocarmé. At the time, there were no tests available that could detect poison in a corpse aside from the procedure developed by British chemist James Marsh that detected arsenic but unfortunately destroyed more fragile plant alkaloids such as nicotine.

Bruising, burns and cuts on Gustave Fougnies's face and attempts by the Comte and Comtesse to clean the body and area with vinegar had already cast suspicion on his death. Pure nicotine is corrosive, which accounted for the burns on Fougnies's face, and police subsequently found vats of pure nicotine and **evidence** of experiments with it on animals in the Comte de Bocarmé's barn. This evidence was, however, only circumstantial so the magistrate consulted the country's leading chemist,

Jean Servais Stas. Stas experimented for three months on organ tissue taken from Fougnies's body and finally managed to extract the liquid nicotine from those tissues using a method involving ethanol, acetic acid and ether. This Stas–Otto method, although since updated, laid the foundations for forensic chemistry and remains a fundamental part of **forensic toxicology** to this day.

The Comte de Bocarmé was sent to the guillotine, but this did not deter future nicotine murderers. In 2010, Paul Curry of Kansas was finally **charged** with the murder of his wife Linda by nicotine poisoning sixteen years after she died and was later **sentenced** to life in jail. Also in 2010, Morgan Mengel of Pennsylvania tried to kill her husband with Snapple™ laced with nicotine but ended up goading her lover to bludgeon him to death with a shovel. The problem with nicotine as a poison is that, although fast acting, it is difficult to administer in the right **lethal** dose and is difficult to hide in food. This did not deter trained chemist Agatha Christie from using it in her 1934 novel *Three Act Tragedy* (published in the US as *Murder in Three Acts*), nor P. D. James in her 1971 novel *Shroud for a Nightingale*.

N

nights
Police night duty or shift that starts at 10 p.m. (UK police slang).

night-vision device
Any electro-optical device used to detect visible and infra-red energy and provide a visible image. ▶ **night-vision goggles** Electro-optical device that detects visible and near-infrared energy, intensifies the energy and thereby provides a visible image for night viewing.

nim

To steal (UK thieves' **cant**, historical slang).

9

9 mm **handgun** (UK/US contemporary slang). ▶ **9 Mike Mike** 9 mm **handgun** (US contemporary gang slang).

ninja

Drug cop in the area (US contemporary gang slang).

Ninja Turtles

Prison guards dressed in full riot gear, also known as 'hats and bats' (US contemporary slang).

nipp

To cheat (UK thieves' **cant**, historical slang).

nob in the fur trade

Barrister (UK Victorian slang).

NOC

See **non-official cover**.

nonce

Prison term for **paedophile** sex-crime offenders who are usually kept segregated from other prisoners for their own safety as they are considered at risk of attack. The term is of unknown origin but one theory is that it is derived from the acronym NONCE, which stands for 'Not On Normal Communal Exercise' and was marked on the door of sex offenders' **cells** so that prison staff would not inadvertently open them while other prisoners' cell doors were also unlocked. Another theory is that it is derived from a

Lincolnshire dialectical word 'nonse', meaning good-for-nothing. A 1984 entry in the *Oxford English Dictionary* extracted from the *Police Review* states that it is derived from 'nancy-boy.' (UK contemporary slang).

non-lethal weapon

Weapon or device that is explicitly designed and primarily used to incapacitate immediately while minimising fatalities, permanent injury to people and undesired damage to property in the target area or environment.

non-official cover (NOC)

Term used by the **Central Intelligence Agency** to describe **case officers** who operate overseas outside the usual diplomatic **cover**.

non-proliferation

Actions taken to prevent the acquisition of **weapons of mass destruction** by preventing or impeding access to **sensitive** technologies, material and expertise as well as their distribution.

Nordic noir

See **Scandi noir**.

Norfolk capon

Distraction or red herring (UK thieves' **cant**, historical slang).

Norway neckcloth

Name for the pillory, the wooden frame with holes for the head and hands of the offenders who were placed in it to receive public abuse. It was also known as the penance board (UK thieves' **cant**, historical slang).

Novichok

Novichok is a group of **nerve agents** that were developed by Soviet Russia in 1971–93 as part of a programme code-named 'Foliant'. The Russian scientists who developed them claim they are the deadliest ever made. Novichok has never been employed for military purposes but was famously used in the **poisoning** of former Russian military officer and **double agent** Sergei Skripal and his daughter Yulia in Salisbury, UK, in March 2018. Skripal and his daughter survived, but Dawn Sturgess, a woman who came into contact with the discarded perfume bottle that was used to contain the Novichok, later died.

NPAS

See **National Police Air Service**.

nubbing cheat

Gallows. ▶ **nubbing-cove** Hangman (UK thieves' **cant**, historical slang).

nunnery

Brothel (UK thieves' **cant**, historical slang).

O

ob, obo, obbo

Abbreviations of observation, meaning under **covert surveillance** by the police (contemporary UK slang).

Official Secrets Act

The Official Secrets Act 1989 came into force on 1 March 1990 in the UK and, among other provisions, made it an offence to disclose any official information without lawful authority. The 1989 Act created offences associated with the **unauthorised disclosure** of information in the following categories: security and **intelligence**, defence, international relations, crime and special **investigation** powers, information resulting from authorised disclosures or entrusted in confidence, and information entrusted in confidence to or by other states or international organisations.

In creating offences under these categories, the Act distinguishes between current and former employees of the security and intelligence services, and crown servants (e.g. ministers, civil servants, members of the police and armed forces) or government contractors. For crown servants and government contractors, the Act stipulates that they can only be found guilty of an offence if the unauthorised disclosure is deemed 'damaging'. Provisions relating to members of the security and intelligence services, on the other hand, stipulate that any unauthorised disclosure relating to security and intelligence is an offence. The maximum penalty for individuals guilty of an offence under the Act is two years' imprisonment or a fine, or both.

officer in charge (OIC)

The officer in charge, also known as the officer in case, is the **Metropolitan Police** officer who has primary responsibility to carry out an **investigation**. This role can change through the life cycle of an investigation, but the police aim to keep the same person in charge as they are also responsible for communication with witnesses and victims, although their role is primarily investigative.

OG

Original gang member (US contemporary gang slang).

omertà

Old rule or law of silence in the **Mafia**, which is mostly no longer upheld by the younger generation of gangsters.

187

To kill someone (often seen in graffiti, US contemporary gang slang).

one time

Police officer, cop (US contemporary gang slang).

on-scene commander

In the US, the federal officer designated to direct federal crisis and consequence management efforts at the scene of a terrorist or **weapons of mass destruction** incident.

operations officer (OO)

An operations officer within the **Central Intelligence Agency** may be involved in **clandestine** activities, and spotting, assessing, developing, recruiting and handling **assets** or individuals with access to vital **foreign intelligence** across issues of national security. An OO's career can include assignments in the **Directorate of Operations'** key areas of activity. These are **human intelligence** collection, **counterintelligence** and **covert** action related to international terrorism, weapons proliferation, international crime and **drugs trafficking** as well as the capabilities and intentions of rogue nations. Operations officers work mostly overseas on assignments that typically last from two to three years.

order

Written direction of a court or judge to do or refrain from doing certain acts

organised crime

Organised crime describes the activities of a group of people involved in serious criminal activities for what are often substantial profits. Violence can be a feature of organised crime but the main **motive** is usually financial gain, although some groups, such as terrorist groups, are politically or ideologically motivated. Organised crime activities can include **drug trafficking**, **human trafficking**, **cybercrime**, armed **robbery**, **money laundering**, counterfeit goods, counterfeit currency, tax **fraud**, immigration fraud and environmental crime.

Organized Crime Drug Enforcement Task Force
Network of regional task forces in the US that coordinates federal **law enforcement** efforts to combat the national and international organisations that cultivate, process and distribute illicit **drugs**.

original lethal-purpose firearm
Firearm originally manufactured with **lethal** purpose in contrast to weapons **converted** to be capable of live firing with lethal effect.

outfit
Family or clan within the **Mafia**.

over-and-under
Firearm with two **barrels** placed one above the other.

owler
Wool smuggler and runner (UK thieves' **cant**, historical slang).

P

PACE
See **Police and Criminal Evidence Act**.

pack
Brick of **cocaine** or packet of **drugs** (London contemporary gang slang associated with drill music).

padding
Unethical practice of police allegedly adding to a **drugs** haul to secure a conviction (UK police slang).

paedophile
Someone who is sexually attracted to prepubescent children. According to the *Diagnostic and Statistical Manual of Psychiatric Disorders* or DSM, this is defined as children under the age of thirteen, and a person must be a minimum of sixteen years of age and at least five years older than the child for their attraction to be considered paedophilia. Most sexual offenders against children are male with an estimated ratio of 10:1 male to female child molesters, although this may be inaccurate as crimes are often underreported. It is not a crime to be a paedophile but it can lead to criminal activity that includes child sexual abuse, rape, grooming, stalking, child pornography and indecent exposure. Paedophilia is one of the most stigmatised and feared mental disorders, which is considered very difficult, if not impossible, to cure.

pannie
Burglary; 'He did a pannie' (UK Victorian slang).

paper
Money. Originating in the US and popularised by gangsta rappers, this is now in wider use (UK/US contemporary slang). Also for US police, a report.

paper, on
'On paper' means on **probation** or on **parole** (UK/US contemporary slang).

paraquat
Paraquat is an organic compound and herbicide that is **toxic** to humans and animals. In humans, paraquat-**poisoning** symptoms include vomiting, blistering, difficulty breathing, kidney and liver damage, and death from multiple organ failure. It is frequently used as a suicide agent in developing countries because it is cheap and readily available, although it is banned in the European Union and tightly regulated in the US. The Paraquat or Vending Machine Murders in Japan in 1985 remain a popular unsolved true-crime mystery with the suspected serial killer, or killers, still at large.

parental child abduction
Child abduction is when a person takes or sends a child, in the UK one under sixteen years old, from their home or out of their country of residence without the appropriate consent. In the case of parental child abduction, this is a parent without the appropriate consent or

parental responsibility. This sometimes happens in cases of relationship breakdown and can lead to distressing and prolonged court cases, especially when the child has been taken abroad. There are three main types of child abduction. Firstly, when a child is taken overseas without the other parent's consent, this may be a criminal offence under UK law, under Section 1 of the Child Abduction Act 1984, punishable by up to seven years imprisonment. Secondly, there is the offence of wrongful retention, which is committed when a child has been retained in a foreign country following an overseas trip, and this may also be a criminal offence under UK law. Thirdly, there is threat of abduction, which occurs when there is a risk that a child may be taken overseas. Both the International Child Abduction and Contact Unit and the charity Reunite, which runs the International Child Abduction Centre, offer support and advice to affected families in the UK.

parole

Parole is the early release of a prisoner before they have completed their sentence, and is usually subject to supervision and contingent on good behaviour. The word originates from the French *parole*, one meaning of which is promise and began to be used during the Middle Ages for prisoners who kept their word to abide by certain conditions. Prisoners who are given parole are released on **probation**, also known as on licence, under certain conditions, including supervision, in the UK. Parole is granted, or not, after a review of a prisoner by the Parole Board. Parole is only available to prisoners serving four years or more of a fixed term sentence.

patent print

Patent prints are finger-, palm or other prints that are clearly visible to the naked eye and do not require the use of powders, chemicals or UV light to spot them at **crime scenes**. They are often composed of blood, ink or other dark substances, and found on hard surfaces such as walls, door and window frames and paper.

pattered

To be tried in a court of law for a crime or **felony** (UK thieves' **cant**, historical slang).

payload

In **cybercrime**, the payload is the part of the **malware** program that actually executes its designated task.

PC

See **police constable**.

P PCP

Phencyclidine or PCP (the initialism comes from phenylcyclohexylpiperidine), also known as angel dust, hog or peace pills, is an anaesthetic that has hallucinogenic properties. It comes in oil, liquid, powder, crystal or pill form. The oil is yellow while the crystals and powder can range in colour from white to light brown. PCP can be sniffed, swallowed, injected or smoked and can lead to users feeling dreamy and euphoric or, conversely, aggressive, panicky, paranoid and violent. It is addictive and use can result in a severe psychotic state, self-harm, convulsions and suicide. PCP is a Class A drug in the UK and illegal to use, give away or sell.

PCSO
See **police community support officer**.

Peckham Rolex
Electronic tag worn by some prisoners upon release
(London police slang). (See **home detention curfew**.)

peds
Bicycle, often used by **drug** couriers and street gangs for a
swift getaway (London contemporary gang slang associated
with drill music).

peels
Orange jumpsuit worn by prisoners in some prisons and
correctional facilities (US contemporary slang).

pellet
Common name for a small spherical **projectile loaded** in
shot shells. It also refers to a non-spherical projectile used
in some **air guns**.

pen
Prison or jail (London contemporary gang slang associated
with drill music). Also an abbreviation for **penitentiary** (US).

penitentiary
In the US, state or federal prison for serious offenders.

pepper spray
Pepper spray is an incapacitating aerosol spray used in
policing, especially for riot or crowd control. It is also popular with civilians for self-defence although it is only legal
for the police to carry and use it.

persistent agent

Chemical agent that remains able to cause casualties for more than twenty-four hours and up to several days or weeks after it is released.

petechial haemorrhage

A petechial haemorrhage is the tiny red dot or mark that appears as a result of asphyxia by external pressure. It can be caused by strangulation, hanging or smothering. The tell-tale red marks range in size from almost invisible to around 2 mm and often occur in the whites or conjunctiva of the eyes as well as on the skin of the face and head, the mucous membranes inside the mouth and behind the ears. The victim needs to have been alive when the pressure was applied, which means petechial haemorrhages are particularly useful to determine if a hanging was staged or otherwise. Petechial haemorrhages can occur on the face as a result of a cardiac arrest and on the lungs and heart in cases of heatstroke or sudden infant death syndrome (SIDS). They can also occur post-mortem, although the patterns tend to differ to those that occur before death. A pathologist therefore needs to take all the circumstances into account when examining the **evidence**.

peter

Prison **cell** (UK contemporary prison slang).

phishing

The fraudulent practice of sending emails that appear to become from a legitimate source, such as a social networking site, a well-known entity such as eBay, or even a bank. They contain a link which, if clicked, directs the victim to a site that looks very convincing and asks them to verify their account information. This login allows cybercriminals to gather **sensitive** information, which enables them to carry out **cybercrime** such as emptying the account of the person concerned.

phreaking

Phreaking or phone phreaking is the **hacking** of a telecommunications system in order to exploit it by, for example, making international calls or accessing voicemail for malicious purposes. A phreak or phone phreak is someone who hacks into a telecommunications system in this manner. Phreakers often band together to link hacked systems and create their own networks that bring in billions in revenue for them.

Picasso

To slice up someone's face in prison is 'to do a Picasso' (US contemporary prison slang).

pickpocket

Someone who steals money or other valuables from another person's pocket, often through sleight of hand so the victim is not immediately aware.

picture frame

Gallows (UK thieves' **cant**, historical slang).

pinch

To steal money under the pretence of getting change (UK thieves' **cant**, historical slang). Also used in a contemporary sense meaning 'to steal'.

pinched

To get caught by the police or federal **agents** (UK/US slang term).

PIR

See **priority intelligence requirement**.

pistol

Handgun in which the **chamber** is a part of the **barrel**.

plant

To hide stolen goods or secrete something away (UK thieves' **cant**, historical slang). Also used in a contemporary sense to mean to place or hide an incriminating item such as **drugs** on someone to make them appear guilty of a crime.

plug

To stab or to shoot. Also a **drug** contact or drug supply (UK contemporary slang).

poison

Substance capable of causing the illness or death of a person or other living organism when ingested or absorbed. Also, as a verb, to administer poison to a person or animal.

Poison, so often the murder weapon of choice in the golden age of Agatha Christie and Dorothy L. Sayers, is enjoying a resurgence in crime fiction, especially in **cosy mysteries**. This is in part due to true-crime **cases** such as that of Alexander Litvinenko with **polonium** but also to modern toxicology constraints. **Forensic toxicology** tests are only carried out post-mortem if there is **evidence** that suggests foul play. Even then, tests are only carried out for the most common **toxic** substances.

polac

UK abbreviation of 'police accident'; usually a road accident involving a police vehicle.

pole

Gun (London contemporary gang slang associated with drill music).

police

Law enforcement officers empowered by the state to enforce law and order, to protect people and property, and to investigate crime. There are many contemporary slang terms for the police including: feds; 5-0; rozzers; po-po; plod; boys in blue; pigs; jakes; **bobbies**; **the Bill** or Old Bill; peelers (historic slang also derived from Sir Robert Peel).

Police and Criminal Evidence Act (PACE)

The Police and Criminal Evidence (PACE) Act of 1984 is the legislative framework passed by an Act of Parliament under which all police powers in the UK are governed. It provides Codes of Conduct for the way in which those powers are exercised and is the set of rules brought in after the Scarman Report following the Brixton Riots in 1981. It was significantly altered by the Serious Organised Crime and Police Act of 2005, which replaced the then defined powers of **arrest** with general powers of arrest for all offences. Although PACE is meant to establish a balance between police powers and the rights of the general public, it remains controversial. PACE applies not just to police officers but to anyone conducting a criminal **investigation**, including Her Majesty's Revenue and Customs and the Ministry of Defence.

police community support officer (PCSO)

A police community support officer (PCSO, referred to in legislation as a community support officer, CSO) is a civilian who supports regular police officers and supposedly has 'enhanced powers', but in reality is assigned the most mundane tasks including making tea.

police constable (PC)

Police constable is the lowest rank in the UK police, being one below **police sergeant**, although all police officers are, by definition, constables, with the highest-ranking officer being the chief constable. Police constables are usually the frontline officers on the beat as well as performing desk and station duties. They respond to public 999 calls, investigate volume crime (e.g. **burglary**) and take initial action at critical incidents. They also work on neighbourhood teams to target long-term local issues.

police inspector

Ranking above a **police sergeant**, a police inspector is the senior operational officer on call. There is usually just one operational inspector on duty at any one time, overseeing all the police officers on duty and responses to critical incidents. They can call out more senior or specialist officers if necessary. They are also the final internal and external arbiter of police resourcing and response disputes.

Police National Computer (PNC)

The Police National Computer or PNC is used to aid **investigations** and share information of local and national importance. It performs real-time checks on people, property, crime and vehicles as well as on the following: persons wanted for extradition, missing persons, people wanted for

judicial purposes, people or vehicles requiring discreet
checks, and misappropriated, lost or stolen objects sought
for the purposes of seizure or evidential purposes.

police procedural

Subgenre of crime fiction that focuses on the investigative
process from the point of view of the police officers
involved. Unlike the detective novel, this is usually an
ensemble piece based on teamwork that reflects real-life
police methodology.

police ranks US

US states and regions have different police departments with their own rank structures, which often
resemble those in the military. Federal agencies have
their own structures and local **law enforcement**
differs according to the community they serve.
Municipal police departments are most often made up
of the following:

- Police technician: entry-level position that involves
  assisting in follow-up **investigations** of assigned
  cases, issuing citations and enforcing parking laws,
  directing traffic at accident and **crime scenes**,
  preparing paperwork for incident reports, keeping
  records, providing general assistance to the public
  and many other support tasks.
- Police officer/police detective/patrol officer: law
  enforcement officers that are generally most familiar
  to civilians. Most attend a training academy and,
  after graduation, carry out police work including

P

patrols, **arresting** suspects and responding to emergency calls. In some departments such as the New York Police Department (NYPD) and Los Angeles Police Department (LAPD), detectives rank above officers and are additionally ranked third to first.

- Police corporal: next rank up from police officer or detective and is a supervisory role, although the title can also belong to non-supervisory members of a specialist unit.
- Police sergeant: duties are usually one step up from those of a police corporal as they actively investigate internal **complaints** and manage their department as well as supervising their officers, training them and participating in disciplinary matters.
- Police lieutenant: akin to middle managers, liaising between their superiors and the ranks below them to action plans as well as conducting performance reviews and developing their departments. They also work with other law enforcement agencies in the area and act as an ambassador for the police department within their local community.
- Police captain: report directly to the chiefs of police or a deputy police chief. They train staff, prepare budgets, handle hiring and promotions, and are even more visible within their community than Police Lieutenants, running community-policing programmes as well as possibly preparing reports on policing in the community.
- Deputy police chief: usually found in larger municipal law enforcement agencies, a deputy police chief is responsible for the administration of a police

bureau or division. They have the same responsibilities as a police captain but also step in as acting chief of police if required. They also design and implement crime-prevention programmes, oversee budgets, and oversee compliance and resources.

- Chief of police: the top job, these officers oversee all aspects of a police department, develop programmes and procedures, and are responsible for the **deployment** of officers to special investigations. They are usually appointed by elected officials and work closely with mayors and local government officials. As the spokesperson for the police, they address the public and media in crisis situations and are ultimately responsible for any issues or incidents that arise under their watch.

police search advisor (PolSA)

In the UK, a police search advisor is usually a **police sergeant** or of more senior rank and advises a chief officer in relation to **counterterrorism** and other search-related matters. They plan searches, and lead and control search teams as well as train them.

police sergeant

One rank up from a **police constable** in the UK, a sergeant supervises teams of officers, oversees police operations, runs volume-crime (e.g. **burglary**) **investigations**, and takes initial control of critical incidents as well as dealing with management issues. They are also present in **custody** and control rooms. They are the immediate point of contact for the escalation of any issues relating to police responses to incidents.

Police Support Unit (PSU)

A Police Support Unit consists of UK police officers who have been specially trained in public order and riot control. They are comparable to divisional SWAT teams in the US who have received additional tactical training so they can deal with situations beyond those normally experienced by an ordinary officer or patrol officer.

police tape

The tape, also known as law enforcement tape, used to cordon off a **crime scene** or other hazard where **law enforcement** is involved. This comes in a variety of colours, with yellow, yellow-white, yellow-black, red and blue-white all being used.

polonium

Highly radioactive, polonium hit the headlines in 2006 when it was used to murder the Russian defector and former FSB officer, Alexander Litvinenko, who drank a cup of green tea laced with polonium-210. It took him three weeks to die and, on his deathbed, he named Russian President Vladimir Putin as the man behind his murder. A UK public enquiry in 2016 found that two former KGB officers, Andrey Lugovoy and Dmitry Kovtun, who had met with Litvinenko the day he fell ill, were responsible for his death. Both deny involvement. Litvinenko's case was the first recorded **poisoning** using polonium-210. Polonium does not kill immediately, although it is **lethal** in very small doses. Victims suffer the effects of radiation poisoning including hair loss, headaches and diarrhoea before they succumb to heart failure.

PolSA

See **police search advisor**.

polygraph test

Popularly known as a lie detector test, polygraphs are used in both criminal **investigation** and the private sector to determine whether a subject is telling the truth. The test measures specific physiological responses to arousal, including respiration, heart rate and blood pressure, while the subject is asked a series of questions. The problem is that there are no specific physiological indicators of lying and the **Comparison Question Test** used with polygraphs has been shown to be biased against the innocent who cannot think of a lie in response to the control question. The American Polygraph Association claims the test is accurate more than 90 per cent of the time while critics claim it is no more than 70 per cent accurate; some in the legal and scientific professions regard it as little better than flipping a coin. Most courts do not admit polygraph **evidence**, although the method remains popular in crime fiction, films and TV series.

polymorphic virus

Computer **virus** that will change its digital footprint every time it replicates. Antivirus software relies on a constantly updated and evolving database of virus signatures to detect any virus that may have infected a system. By changing its signature upon replication, a polymorphic virus may elude antivirus software, making it very hard to eradicate.

pool bloodstain

Sustained bleeding from a wound or arterial blood loss causes blood to accumulate or pool at a **crime scene**. If there is no victim or body present, the amount of blood present can indicate the seriousness or even the nature of the injury, and whether that is likely to be fatal.

pop a cap

Shoot at someone (US contemporary gang slang).

popp

Pistol (UK thieves' **cant**, historical slang).

posse

Jamaican gang, derived from Spaghetti Westerns (UK/US/Jamaican contemporary gang slang).

preliminary inquiry

Review of the facts and circumstances of an incident or **allegation** to determine if the preliminary information or circumstances are sufficient to warrant the initiation of an **investigation** or referral to an investigative entity.

prigg

Pickpocket (UK thieves' **cant**, historical slang).

primer

Component in **ammunition** which explodes when struck by the **firing pin**, or under an electric excitement, igniting the **propellant** and discharging the **projectile**. The primer is composed of a primer cup containing priming mixture, the composition of which varies according to the firearm and ammunition used. Primers are also used in flares, mortars, hand grenades, rocket-propelled grenades and other larger ammunition components. ▶**primer cup** Brass or copper cup designed to contain priming mixture.

priority intelligence requirement (PIR)
Intelligence requirement that the commander of an operation and staff need to understand the threat and other aspects of the operational environment.

prison
A prison is a building or set of buildings in which people are held while they are awaiting trial for a crime or are being punished for one. In England and Wales, prisoners are categorised based on the likelihood of the risk of escape, the potential harm to the public if they were to escape and their potential to cause a threat to the control and stability of a prison. The rules are different for men, women and young adult offenders. Male prisoners are sent to prisons in one of the following four categories:

- Category A: **high-security prisons** that house prisoners who, if they were to escape, pose the greatest threat to the public, the police or national security.
- Category B: local or training prisons. Local prisons house prisoners who are brought directly from a local court if they have been **sentenced** or are on remand. Training prisons hold long-term and high-security prisoners.
- Category C: training and resettlement prisons. The majority of prisoners are placed in a Category C prison. They provide prisoners with educational and

other opportunities so they can find a job and reintegrate into the community on release.

- Category D: open prisons. These are minimal security prisons that allow eligible prisoners to spend most of their day away from the prison on licence to work, attend education or for other resettlement purposes. Open prisons only house prisoners that have been risk-assessed and deemed suitable for open conditions.

Women and young adults are assessed and categorised according to their needs and potential risks before being held in closed or open prisons. If they are categorised as high risk they are given restricted status and can only be held in a closed prison. In exceptional circumstances, women and young adults can be held in a Category A prison. Prison staff regularly assess prisoners throughout their sentence to ensure they are still in the correct category prison.

In the US, prisoners are similarly assessed based on risk factors and also on needs, including medical needs. It is the responsibility of the Federal Bureau of Prisons to decide where a prisoner will be designated to serve their sentence. Prisons are categorised as Minimum (also known as Federal Prison Camps), Low (Federational Correctional Institutions or FCIs), Medium (can be FCIs or USPs), High (also known as United States Penitentiaries or USPs) or Federational Correctional Complexes (FCCs) where different category institutions are located close to one another. There are also administrative facilities which are institutions with specialist missions such as the detention of pre-trial prisoners, the treatment of inmates with serious or chronic medical problems or the containment of extremely dangerous, violent or escape-prone inmates. Administrative facilities include Metropolitan Correctional Centers (MCCs), Metropolitan Detention Centers (MDCs), Federal Detention Centers (FDCs), Federal Medical Centers (FMCs), the Federal Transfer Center (FTC), the Medical Center for Federal Prisoners (MCFP) and the Administrative-Maximum Security Penitentiary (ADX). Administrative facilities, except the ADX, are capable of holding inmates in all security categories.

prison wolf

Inmate who is straight on the outside but has sexual relationships with other men while in prison (US contemporary slang).

private prison

Otherwise known as contracted prisons, these are run by private companies in the UK. Prisoners in private prisons have the same rights and rules as prisoners in other prisons although the governor is known as a director and prison officers as prison **custody** officers. Currently there are thirteen private prisons in the UK: Altcourse, Ashfield, Bronzefield (for women), Doncaster, Dovegate, Forest Bank, Lowdham Grange, Oakwood, Parc, Peterborough (for men and women), Rye Hill, Thameside and Northumberland.

probation

Probation allows a convicted defendant to be released with a shortened or **suspended sentence** for a specified duration dependent on good behaviour. Probationers are placed under the supervision of a probation officer and must fulfil certain conditions. If the probationer violates a condition of probation, the court may place additional restrictions on the probationer or **order** the probationer to serve a term of imprisonment.

profiling

Profiling, known as criminal or offender profiling, is a combination of **law enforcement** and **forensic** psychology with few boundaries, no agreed methodology and little in the way of agreed definitions or terminology. It is the art and science of **crime scene** analysis, forensic psychology and behavioural science to develop a description of an unknown offender, often a serial offender, and its first use is often cited to be the **case** of **Jack the Ripper**. As well as its application in real-life criminal cases, profiling is a staple of crime fiction, TV series and films including the popular Netflix series *Mindhunter* (2017–) .

P

projectile

Object (**bullet**, **shot**, **slug** or **pellet**) that is **discharged** by the force of rapidly burning gases or by other means when a gun is fired.

projection bloodstain

A projection or projected **bloodstain** or spatter is caused by arterial spurting, **expirated** spatter or blood mixing with air from an internal injury, and blood spatter cast off by an object such as a bullet passing through a blood source. Arterial spurting occurs when a major artery is severed and blood is pushed out by the pumping heart, often forming an arcing pattern consisting of individual stains, one for each pump of the heart. Expirated spatter tends to form a fine mist. Projected blood spatter is the result of a blood source being subjected to an action or force greater than the force of gravity.

propellant

Chemical compound inside a gun **cartridge** which burns rapidly when ignited to produce large amounts of hot gas. This gas drives the **projectile(s)** out of the **barrel**.

psychological thriller

Thriller that focuses on the often unstable and unreliable psychological and emotional states of both victim and protagonist. Moral ambiguity, complex relationships and shifting realities are all hallmarks of the genre.

psychological warfare

Use of threats, propaganda and other psychological techniques to mislead, intimidate, demoralise or otherwise influence the thinking or behaviour of an opponent.

P

pulled

To 'get pulled' is to be stopped by the police. Can also mean taken to one side by a senior officer for a minor **misdemeanour** (US contemporary police and UK general slang).

pump

Shotgun (US contemporary gang slang).

pump action

Manual repeating **action** of a **firearm** where all the mechanisms are moved by the back and forward action of the sliding fore-end (the pump), which ejects the spent shell, cocks the hammer and loads a new shell in the **chamber**. By then pushing the slide forward, the shooter pushes the block and **firing pin** into the firing position. This action is repeated every time the gun is fired.

puppy, dog
Gun (US/Jamaican contemporary gang slang).

push, pusha, pushy
Bicycle, often used by **drug** couriers and street gangs for a swift getaway (London contemporary gang slang associated with drill music).

Q

Queen's evidence (QE)
If a criminal turns QE then they give **evidence** against **accomplices** in exchange for what they hope is a lighter **sentence**.

queer bitt
Counterfeit money (UK thieves' **cant**, historical slang).

queer coal makers
Counterfeiters of coins (UK thieves' **cant**, historical slang).

queer popp
Bad **pistol** (UK thieves' **cant**, historical slang).

R

rabbit

Prison inmate who has a history of escape attempts or is planning to escape (US contemporary slang). Also the target in an **intelligence surveillance** operation.

Rader, Dennis

Dennis Rader (b. 1945) was the seemingly devoted family man and churchgoer who was also known as BTK, or the BTK killer, because he would bind, torture and kill his victims. He carried out ten murders in Wichita, Kansas, between 1974 and 1991, taunting the authorities with correspondence and clues. Rader liked to strangle his victims before taking souvenirs from the scenes of his crimes, although he also shot and stabbed them. He derived sexual pleasure from killing, leaving his semen at the scene of his first crime where he killed four members of the Otero family. He later placed a letter in a book in the local library where he admitted to their killings and wrote, 'It's hard to control myself. You probably call me "psychotic with sexual perversion hang-up".' He added that he would strike again, stating, 'The code words for me will be bind them, torture them, kill them, B.T.K.' From then on he was known as the BTK killer and carried on terrorising Wichita, sending poems and letters to local newspapers and TV stations, and even calling the police to report a homicide he carried out in 1977. After his final murder in 1991 BTK seemed to disappear as Rader focused on his work, family and roles as president of his church council and Boy Scout leader. Then, in 2004, with the thirtieth anniversary of the Otero killings and attendant publicity, Rader could not resist once more taunting the authorities, sending word puzzles, letters and even an outline for a BTK story to them as well as to local media. He also dropped off packages containing clues, one of which included a computer disc that led the authorities to Rader's church. They noticed his white van on **CCTV** covering the places where he had dropped off packages and matched him to **crime scenes** through **DNA** taken from his daughter. Rader was **arrested** in 2005 and admitted to all his crimes, and is serving ten life **sentences** for his murders. His story inspired Stephen King's novella *A Good Marriage* (2010), an episode of Netflix's *Mindhunter* (2017–) and the movie *BTK* (2008).

Rambo

Large knife (London contemporary gang slang associated with drill music). Also, 'doing a Rambo' is carrying out an armed **assault** or attack (US contemporary gang slang).

Ramsay

Large knife, named after well-known UK chef Gordon Ramsay (London contemporary gang slang associated with drill music).

rankin

High-ranking member of a gang (US/Jamaican contemporary gang slang).

rape

Rape is defined in the UK as a person intentionally penetrating another person's vagina, anus or mouth with a penis without the other person's consent. **Assault** by penetration is when a person penetrates another person's vagina or anus with any part of the body other than a penis, or by using an object, without the person's consent. See also **sexual assault**.

rapper
Perjurer (UK thieves' **cant**, historical slang).

rat
Snitch or **informant**. Used by the US **Mafia** and other gangs. To 'rat someone out' means to snitch or inform on them.

rate of fire
Number of **projectiles** that can be **discharged** from the **firearm** in a given timeframe such as a minute.

raven
Male operative engaged in Russian **sexpionage** (see **swallow**).

R

raw intelligence
Colloquial term meaning collected **intelligence** information that has not yet been converted or processed into finished intelligence.

raze up
Cut with a razor (UK contemporary prison slang).

reactivation
Restoration of a previously **deactivated weapon**'s capacity to fire. Common in the illicit trade and trafficking of guns to avoid or subvert import and other restrictions.

receiver

Someone who receives stolen goods. Also the basic unit of a **firearm** that houses the firing and breech mechanism and onto which the **barrel** and **stock** are assembled. In **revolvers**, **pistols** and break-open guns, it is called the frame.

recoil

Backward force of a **firearm** caused by expansion of powder gases that also expels the **bullet** out of the **barrel**.

reconnaissance

Mission undertaken to obtain, by visual observation or other methods, information about the activities and resources of an enemy or adversary, or about the geographic and other characteristics of a particular area or facility.

reloading

Reassembling a fired **cartridge case** with a new **primer**, **propellant** and **bullet** or **wadding** and **shot** (see **hand-loading**); or simply re-arming a discharged weapon, e.g. by inserting a new **magazine**.

R

Remington 870

Pump-action shotgun that is the bestselling shotgun of all time. There are specific variants made for police and **law enforcement** including the Police model, which is fitted with a police-specific walnut or synthetic **stock** and is shortened to fit a vehicle-mounted rack and to allow for quick visual inspection of the **magazine**. Police models have Remington 870 Police Magnum stamped on the **receiver**. Remington also make a Marine model and the MCS (Modular Combat Shotgun) version of the 870.

replica gun

Functional reproduction of an existing **firearm** (see **imitation firearm**). It is also the term used to refer to a modern reproduction of an **antique firearm**.

restricted target

Valid target, whether that is a person or a place, that has specific restrictions placed on the actions that are authorised against it due to operational considerations.

resurrection man

Grave robber who stole bodies for surgeons (UK thieves' **cant**, historical slang).

revolver

Firearm, usually a **handgun** with a revolving **cylinder** of **chambers**, arranged to allow several successive shots to be **discharged** by the same firing mechanism without **reloading**.

RIC

Remand in **custody** (UK police acronym).

Richard Roe

The name Richard Roe or the surname Roe are used in court cases when two parties must remain anonymous, most famously in the US Supreme Court case of **Roe vs Wade**. The female version is Jane Roe. See also **Jane/ John Doe**.

ricin

Ricin has been described as 'the perfect **poison**', largely because its key ingredient, castor beans, is so easily obtainable, as are instructions on how to extract the **lethal** poison from the beans under non-laboratory conditions. Once properly prepared, it only takes a pinhead-sized amount of ricin to kill and there is no known antidote. Ricin acts by shutting down the liver and other organs if ingested or by causing respiratory failure if inhaled. It was notoriously used in the 1978 murder of Bulgarian journalist Georgi Markov in London, who was injected with a ricin **pellet** fired from an umbrella. In 2002, there was an alleged plot to attack the London Underground with ricin. This was known as the Wood Green ricin plot. The suspect contaminated articles recovered were sent to the Biological Weapon Identification Group at the Defence Science and Technology Laboratory at Porton Down in Wiltshire. There was no trace of ricin on any of them, a fact that was suppressed for over two years. Ricin-tainted letters have been sent to former US President Barack Obama, former New York Mayor Michael Bloomberg, federal judges and the Pentagon. These were laced with a crude form of homemade ricin that was not weapons grade.

ride, ride my bang

Prison spell or **sentence**, time spent in prison (UK contemporary prison slang).

ride on

Go to another gang area or turf to attack them, usually in vehicles (US contemporary gang slang).

ride with

A prison inmate doing favours for another inmate, including sexual favours, in return for protection, items from the prison commissary or contraband (US contemporary slang).

rifle

Firearm with a rifled **barrel**.

rifling

Spiral or helicoidal **grooves** inside the **barrel** of a gun
designed to make the **bullet** spin, thereby stabilising it and
improving its accuracy. Rifling leaves unique marks on a
bullet that can be an aid to **forensic ballistics**.

rigor mortis

Rigor mortis is the stiffening of the body after death
that results from the loss of adenosine triphosphate
(ATP) from the muscles. Rigor usually starts around
two hours after death and spreads at the same time
throughout the body, although the smaller muscles,
such as those in the face and neck, are affected first.
This initial stiffening of the facial muscles leads to the
characteristic grimace often reported by **scenes of
crime officers**. The initial stage of rigor, known as the
rigid stage, lasts from eight to twelve hours, and once
the body is completely stiff it stays that way for up to
another eighteen hours. The muscles then start to lose
their stiffness, working in reverse with the largest
muscles relaxing first followed by the smaller ones until
the entire body is once more flaccid. Because of these
scales, rigor mortis is a good method of predicting time
of death, although environmental factors such as
temperature have to be taken into account.

ring

Bullet (US/Jamaican contemporary gang slang).

R

robbery

Taking or **attempting** to take something of value from its rightful owner or possessor by force, or threat of force or violence, and/or by putting the victim in fear.

Rohypnol

Rohypnol (a brand name for flunitrazepam) suppresses the central nervous system and is a type of benzodiazepine. Like other **drugs** in this family, it is a muscle relaxant that lowers inhibitions and causes amnesia. For this reason, it is frequently used as a **date-rape** drug, especially as it intensifies the effects of **alcohol** and other drugs such as **heroin** and **cocaine**. Rohypnol can be detected in urine up to three days after ingestion. Street names include: circle; roofie; roach; rope; ropie; roopie; rophy; ruffie; Mexican Valium.

rolling-car pickup

In **spy** lingo, a **clandestine** car pickup of a person or object executed so smoothly that the car hardly stops at all and appears to have simply kept moving.

Romeo spy

Man, usually an **intelligence officer**, **agent** or investigator, whose job it is to seduce women who have access to confidential material, in the hope that through pillow talk the women will reveal secrets. Romeo spies were created out of practicality in the Cold War, representing a cost-effective opportunity to steal West German political, military and security secrets that was spotted by Markus Wolf, chief **foreign intelligence** officer for East Germany's Stasi or secret police.

R

Wolf was so good at his job that, for twenty years, Western intelligence did not even know what he looked like and he was dubbed the 'Man Without a Face'. He believed that one woman with the right contacts and motivation could provide more secrets than ten diplomats, and he was right. Wolf deployed young, clean-cut men who usually pretended to be carrying out some kind of humanitarian work or mission, targeting well-educated, upper middle-class women with access to the information the Stasi required, often working for the West German government. The Romeo spies, who had to pass a rigorous screening process, were schooled on the likes, dislikes and vulnerabilities of their targets, and engineered supposedly chance encounters to meet them. They then proceeded skilfully to seduce them into relationships with good manners and old-fashioned charm.

Despite advertising campaigns warning of these young men, many women fell for them and began relationships, although most subsequently ended those relationships when the Romeo spies moved on to the next stage of their mission and asked the women to **spy** or pass on secrets to them. Some, however, agreed and their **espionage**, along with their relationships, lasted for decades. The Romeo spies were forbidden to marry their targets because the West German government carried out background checks on any potential spouse of someone who had access to state secrets, but many also fell for their Juliets. Those who did were sometimes removed back to East Germany, never to be seen by their target again, or suffered an untimely 'accidental' death.

Many of the women also fell in love with their Romeos and some fell in love with espionage itself, carrying on even when their Romeo left or was replaced. The Romeo spies programme ended in early 1990 when German reunification became inevitable and the Stasi destroyed all documents relating to it. Markus Wolf escaped to Moscow, where he had grown up and learned his **tradecraft**, but surrendered three years later on the Bavarian border and was **sentenced** to six years in prison for treason. He was later pardoned on the grounds that East Germany was a sovereign state when he worked for it and he was therefore entitled to carry out espionage on behalf of that state. He died at the age of eighty-three on 9 November 2006, the seventeenth anniversary of the fall of the Berlin Wall.

rootkit

Malware program that is installed on a system through various means, including the same methods that allow **viruses** to be injected into a system such as email, downloading unsafe programs or files, and websites designed to introduce malware. Once a rootkit is introduced it creates a **back door** that will allow remote, unauthorised entry. A rootkit is installed and functions at such low system levels that it can be designed to erase its own tracks and activity from the now vulnerable system, allowing a **hacker** or **cracker** to navigate through entire networks without being exposed. Rootkits can be directly installed from a CD or USB drive to a system that is not normally remotely accessible, sometimes by means of **social engineering**. Rootkits are especially dangerous as they are so difficult to spot.

R

round

Generic term for a **bulleted cartridge**.

RTA

Road traffic accident (UK police acronym).

rub down

Search of a prison **cell** (UK contemporary prison slang).

ruffler

Handcuffs (UK thieves' **cant**, historical slang).

rush

Immediate and intense surge in sensation felt when smoking or injecting a **drug**. The rush varies in length depending on the drug. Also, to attack (US contemporary gang slang).

rush-in

Restrain or confine a prisoner in their **cell** before moving them (UK contemporary prison slang).

RVP

Rendezvous point (UK police acronym).

S

SAD
See **Special Activities Division**.

safe house
Apparently innocuous or unremarkable house or premises established by an organisation in order to facilitate **clandestine** or **covert** activity in relative security. Safe houses may be used as a refuge for **agents**, defectors, couriers, escapees or evaders, for rendezvous, training, briefing or questioning, or for storage of supplies and equipment. They also act as a place of safety where police witnesses or victims of crime are taken for their own protection.

safety device
Mechanical device in a **firearm** designed to block the firing mechanism during the movement of the mobile parts to prevent unintentional **discharge** when the weapon is properly engaged.

safing
When applied to weapons and **ammunition**, the changing from a state of readiness for use to a safe condition. Also known as de-arming.

samurai
Large knife or samurai-style sword (London contemporary gang slang associated with drill music).

sanitise

To revise a report or other document in such a way as to prevent identification of **sources**, or of the actual people and places with which it is concerned, or of the way in which it was acquired. Sanitisation usually involves deleting or substituting names and other key information.

SAR

See **Suspicious Activity Report**.

sarin

Sarin was developed in 1937 by the German chemist Gerhard Schrader as an insecticide but the Nazis quickly realised it was more **lethal** than the chlorine gas they had used up until then in **chemical weapons**. So fearful were they of its effects and the possible retaliatory consequences, they did not use it in the Second World War but the Iraqis did in 1988, killing 5,000 Kurds. Sarin became infamous thanks to the 1995 Tokyo subway attack in which a doomsday cult, Aum Shinrikyo, released it during rush hour, killing twelve people and injuring hundreds more. A thirteenth victim died after fourteen years in hospital. Odourless and tasteless, sarin works by turning our own nervous systems against us, resulting in convulsions, paralysis and death within minutes if the dose is sufficient.

sawn-off shotgun

Shotgun that has had its **barrel** and/or **stock** shortened.

scamp foot

Street robber, **footpad** or spicer (UK thieves' **cant**, historical slang).

Scandi noir

The long, dark Scandinavian winters have spawned a swathe of crime fiction, TV series and films known collectively as Scandi or Nordic noir. The murders are brutal; the outlook bleak. Ice-hard detectives crack in the face of their demons and sacrifice all for what becomes a personal crusade. Their colleagues are their family. Frost forms over lonely hearts. The police hero or heroine aches with a longing that can never be fulfilled. There are monsters to be tracked across snow-fields and hunted down in urban wastelands while Scandinavian society turns a blind eye. The morals and motivations are complex, the plotlines international. Relentlessly realistic and pared to the bone, Scandi noir reflects the darkest recesses of our souls.

scene of crime examiner (SCE)

A scene of crime examiner or crime scene examiner (scene examiner in Scotland) is usually, although not always, a civilian **forensic** specialist who attends a **crime scene**, or the scene of a major accident or incident, to search it methodically and collect any **evidence** they find, which they record and preserve. They will look for **fingerprints**, footprints, **DNA** and any other forensic evidence, and will also photograph or video the scene and the evidence they collect. The evidence is then sent or submitted to laboratories for analysis. They are normally based at police headquarters or divisional stations and sometimes in dedicated forensic facilities. They are also known as forensic investigators, **scenes of crime officers** and, especially in the US, as crime scene investigators (CSIs).

S

scenes of crime officer (SOCO)

A scenes of crime officer finds, records and gathers **forensic evidence** at a **crime scene** as well as preserving it for the police. SOCOs are not usually police officers but are employed by the police. They are also known by some forces as crime scene investigators, **scene of crime examiners** or forensic scene investigators.

SCO19

See **Specialist Firearms Command**.

scram

Gun (London contemporary gang slang associated with drill music).

screw

Prison officer (UK contemporary prison slang).

search warrant

Legal authorisation or court **order** issued by a judge or magistrate for a police officer or other official to search a property, person, vehicle or premises, and to seize any **evidence** they find. In most countries, search warrants are only issued to facilitate criminal **investigations** and not for civil cases.

secret writing

The official **Federal Bureau of Investigation** definition for this is invisible writing. This can be any **tradecraft** technique that involves invisible messages hidden in, or on, apparently innocuous materials, including invisible inks, microdots and numerous other variations. It can additionally be defined as the use of special inks, also known as the

S

'wet system', or **carbon** papers, also known as the 'dry system' within tradecraft.

securing a crime scene

It is the job of the first officer or responder at a **crime scene** to secure it by setting up a cordon, having first prioritised the preservation of life, taken notes of the names of all people at the scene, and considered and recorded the **contamination** risks to **forensic evidence**. They do so by identifying the extent of the scene and setting cordons; controlling access to the scene; covering it if necessary to protect it from the elements and inclement weather; requesting specialist assistance; and then creating a log of the scene, recording all people, police, vehicles and other agencies who attend the scene from outside the cordon, along with the date and time of arrival and departure, and reason for visit. The first officer or **first responder** also records any initial actions taken to preserve the integrity of evidence. The subsequent highest-ranking officer who attends the scene assumes the role of supervisor, ensures that the above actions have been carried out and that any emergency preservation of the scene is performed as necessary. They also establish a rendezvous point at the outer cordon and communicate this point to all staff in order that they can report to the crime scene loggist on arrival at the scene.

S

security service

Organisation or department of a government charged with responsibility for **espionage**, **counterespionage** or internal security functions. **MI5**'s formal title is the Security Service.

self-radicalisation

Process a person follows to advocate or adopt an extreme belief system for the purpose of facilitating or conducting ideologically based violence, or terrorism, to advance political, religious or social change. The self-radicalised individual has not been recruited by other violent extremists but may seek out direct or indirect contact with other violent extremists for moral or other support and to boost his or her extremist beliefs.

semi-automatic firearm

Self- or auto-loading **firearm** that fires a single shot when the **trigger** is pulled, the fired **cartridge case** is ejected, and a fresh cartridge **loaded** into the **chamber**. The trigger must be released and pulled again to fire another shot.

senior investigating officer (SIO)

In the UK, a detective, usually ranked **detective chief inspector** or above, appointed to lead an investigation into a major crime, and thereby responsible for the management of strategy, resources and procedures.

sensitive

When applied to a document, activity, programme, place, person or some kind of information this means it needs protection from disclosure that could cause embarrassment, compromise or a threat to security. ▶ **sensitive site** Designated, geographically limited area with particular diplomatic, informational, military, economic, national or state sensitivity.

sentence

Punishment given to a person convicted of a crime. A sentence is ordered by the judge, based on the verdict of the jury (or the judge's decision if there is no jury), within the possible punishments set by law. A sentence is popularly thought of as the jail or prison time ordered after conviction. Technically, a sentence includes all fines, community service, restitution or other punishment, or terms of **probation**.

serial number

In weaponry, a number applied to a **firearm** by the manufacturer in order to identify the individual firearm.

serve

To beat someone up badly (US contemporary gang slang).

sex offender register

When a person is convicted or cautioned in relation to a sexual offence, or has committed a sexual offence but been found not guilty due to insanity or a disability in the UK, they are added to the Violent and Sex Offender Register (ViSOR). In the US, there is also a central Sex Offender Registry (SOR).

sexpionage

Use of sex, seduction, romance or a relationship, or the promise of any of those, to carry out **espionage**. It has been a time-honoured trick up a **spy**'s sleeve, or elsewhere, since the days of Mata Hari, the Dutch exotic dancer and courtesan who was convicted of spying for the Germans during the First World War and executed by firing squad, and well before that. **Spies** have used sexpionage to blackmail, elicit secrets and lure valuable **sources** into relationships and even marriage (see **honey trap**, **Romeo spy**, **swallow** and **raven**).

sexual assault

Sexual or indecent **assault** is a sexual act inflicted on someone without their consent that causes physical, psychological and emotional violation. It can involve forcing or manipulating someone to witness or participate in any sexual acts. Not all cases of sexual assault involve violence, cause physical injury or leave visible marks but are not less serious for that.

▶ **sexual assault kit (SAK)** Envelope, box or other container that includes items for collecting and preserving materials including fibres, hairs and bodily fluids that may provide **evidence** from sexual assault victims, the **accused** or suspects in sexual assault **cases**.

shank

To stab, to **assault** someone with a knife, dagger or similar sharp object. It can also refer to a homemade knife or weapon, usually fashioned out of something that is not ordinarily used as a knife, e.g. the end of a toothbrush filed down until it is sharp. When used in prison it means to stab with a homemade knife (contemporary slang).

shellin'

Shooting (London contemporary gang slang associated with drill music).

Shipman, Harold

Harold Frederick Shipman (1946–2004) was a GP nicknamed Doctor Death as the UK's, and one of the world's, most prolific serial killers. Shipman is believed to have killed at least 218 of his mostly elderly female patients with **lethal** injections of diamorphine between 1975 and

1998 in Hyde, Greater Manchester, where he practised at a medical centre. Detectives believe the total could be closer to 250 although Shipman was only found guilty of 15 specimen murders at Preston Crown Court in 2000. Shipman had been caught forging prescriptions of Demerol for his own use in 1975 and was required to attend a **drug** rehabilitation programme. Over the years, people became suspicious of the high mortality rate among his patients, but the police dismissed the concerns of those at Shipman's medical centre and a local funeral home who were suspicious about the high number of Shipman's elderly female patients who were being cremated. The subsequent Shipman Inquiry in 2005 blamed the force for assigning inexperienced officers to the **case**. It was only when he was caught forging the will of Kathleen Grundy in 1998 in an attempt to defraud her estate of £360,000 that Shipman was finally apprehended. His attempted **fraud** along with the abnormally high mortality rate at his practice made detectives look closer and the body of Kathleen Grundy was exhumed and found to contain traces of diamorphine. Shipman never confessed to his crimes and insisted Grundy had been an addict, but computer **evidence** showed that he had written up his medical notes about her after her death. Shipman hanged himself in Wakefield prison in 2004, on the eve of his fifty-eighth birthday, apparently to ensure that his wife Primrose would receive his full NHS pension. The Shipman Inquiry revealed some of the extent of his crimes, with his youngest suspected victim having been only four years old. It also led to changes in standard medical and funeral procedures in the UK.

S

shiv

Knife, razor or other sharp weapon fashioned out of something that is already sharp or lends itself to the purpose, and often homemade in prison. To shiv means to slash, stab or cut someone with the aforementioned sharp object (contemporary slang).

shooty

Shotgun (US/Jamaican contemporary gang slang).

shoplifter

Someone who steals items and goods from shops (UK thieves' **cant**, historical slang and still in contemporary use).

Short-Range Agent Communication (SRAC)

Device or gadget that allows an **intelligence agent** and their **case officer** to communicate secretly over a short distance.

shot

Small **pellets** of varying sizes and weights that are used as the **projectiles** in **shotgun cartridges**. ▶**shotgun** A **firearm** with a **smooth bore**, normally designed to be fired from the shoulder and which usually **discharges** a **cartridge** containing a number of small **pellets** or **shot** or a single solid **slug** or any other **load** that can be carried by the cartridge. ▶**shotgun cartridge** Centrefire or rimfire cartridge **loaded** with small-diameter **shot**. ▶**shot size** Numerical or alphabetical designation related to the average diameter of a **pellet**. The number system varies from country to country.

shotter

drug dealer (UK contemporary slang).

show me your back

'Leave or get lost' (US contemporary gang slang).

side-by-side

Firearm with two **barrels** arranged adjacently in the horizontal plane.

signal

In **spy** lingo this means any form of **clandestine tradecraft** that uses a system of marks, signs or **codes** for signalling between operatives. ▶ **signal site** Prearranged fixed location, usually in a public place, on which an **agent** or **intelligence officer** can place a predetermined mark in order to alert another agent or officer to the commencement or termination of operational activity. This might be something like a chalk mark on a lamppost or a tiny piece of tape stuck to a particular wall.

sign-of-life signal

Signal emitted periodically to confirm that an **intelligence agent** or officer is safe.

S

SIG Sauer P226

Full-size **semi-automatic pistol** popular with military and **law enforcement** services across the world including the SAS, US Navy SEALs, the British Army, the **Federal Bureau of Investigation** and multiple US police forces such as the NYPD and the Texas Rangers. Made of steel, it comes in 9 mm, .357 SIG or .40 S&W varieties with a longer-than-average barrel that gives it better ballistic performance and accuracy.

single action

In relation to **firearms**, this means the **hammer** must be pulled back manually or **cocked** prior to utilising the **trigger** to operate the firing mechanism.

single shot

Firearm without a **magazine**, holding a single **round** of **ammunition**.

SIO

See **senior investigating officer**.

skaghead

Heroin addict (contemporary slang).

skeng

Gun (London contemporary slang associated with drill music).

skewer

Sword (UK thieves' **cant**, historical slang).

skinner

Kidnapper of boys and men who are then forced to enlist in the army (UK thieves' **cant**, historical slang).

sleeper

In **intelligence** terms an **illegal agent** in a foreign country, or placed in particular territory, who does not engage in intelligence activities until activated or told to do so.

sleeving

Practice common in gun conversions by criminals to over-
come weaknesses in a **barrel** caused by the presence of
venting holes or in an attempt to provide a barrel that
chambers available **ammunition** correctly. It involves
replacing an existing gun barrel with a metal tube or to
inserting a tube inside a weak barrel.

slide action

Repeating mechanism in a gun where the **loading** is done
by moving a part of the **firearm** parallel to the **barrel**. Also
called **pump action**.

slopping out

Manual removal of human waste from a prison **cell**,
normally carried out by prisoners, where there are no toilet
facilities in a cell. Buckets or chamber pots are used
instead. The practice is now considered unsanitary and
degrading, and is banned in prisons in the UK. There have
been reports of the practice continuing in English prisons
due to a lack of in-cell sanitary provision.

slug

Unique **projectile** in a **shotgun cartridge**.

small arms

According to NATO's definition, these are individual **firearms** capable of being carried by one person and fired without mechanical support. They, especially but not exclu-
sively, include **handguns**, shoulder weapons, light
machine guns, **sub-machine guns** and **assault rifles**.

smasher
Passer of bad or counterfeit money (UK thieves' **cant**, historical slang).

smashing queer screens
Passing forged notes (UK Victorian slang).

SMG
See **Sub-machine gun**.

smooth bore
Firearm with a **barrel** with no internal **rifling**, typically a **shotgun**.

snakesman
Child sent into a house through a small opening such as a window to let burglars in (UK historical slang).

snapper
Pistol (UK thieves' **cant**, historical slang).

sneak
Petty **thief** of small articles. A morning sneak would go down to the servants' quarters just as they were up and busy in the kitchen and steal whatever they could find. They would also do the same in shops as they opened. An evening sneak would so the same at closing up time (UK thieves' **cant**, historical slang). From this we get the contemporary sneak thief who steals small items after entering through open doors or reaching through open windows.

snowing
Stealing the washing from a line (UK historical slang).

SO

See **special operations**.

social engineering

In relation to **cybercrime**, social engineering means to deceive someone for the purpose of acquiring sensitive and personal information such as credit-card details or usernames and passwords. This can be by means of a telephone call purporting to come from your bank or ISP (Internet Service Provider) informing you, say, of new username and password guidelines being implemented by the company, and asking you to reveal your current ones so they can be changed. Social engineering is very convincing and works on even sophisticated users of systems.

SOCO

See **scenes of crime officer**.

soft-point bullet

Semi-jacketed **bullet** where a portion of the core is exposed at the nose of the bullet.

sound moderator

Also known as a sound suppressor or a silencer. A device that attaches to, or is permanently fixed to, the **muzzle** of the **barrel** of a **firearm** and reduces the noise or report produced by a discharging **cartridge**.

source

In **intelligence** and policing terms, a person, thing or activity from whom or from which information or services are obtained.

spam

Spam is unsolicited email, otherwise known as junk email. Spammers gather or buy lists of email addresses, which they use to bombard users with this unsolicited mail. Usually these emails are simply advertising a product or service but sometimes they can be used for **phishing** and/ or to direct someone to websites or products that will introduce **malware** into their system. Most mail services have spam filters and these should be employed whenever possible. Spam emails should be deleted immediately and the links they contain should never be clicked.

speak

To rob or take away. 'He's been spoken to' means he has been taken by the police or is dead (UK thieves' **cant**, historical slang).

Special Activities Division (SAD)

The Special Activities Division (SAD) of the **Central Intelligence Agency** carries out **clandestine** activities and operations through two divisions: the Political Action Group (PAG) and the Special Operations Group (SOG).

special agent

Detective or investigator who works for the federal government in the US, most famously for the **Federal Bureau of Investigation**. Operatives who work for the **Central Intelligence Agency** in **clandestine intelligence** are not known as special or secret **agents** but as officers.

Specialist Firearms Command (SCO19)

This is the **Metropolitan Police Service**'s specialist **firearms** unit. SCO19 deals with any armed incident in

London. It consists of around 550 members, male and female, including training staff, Counter Terrorist Specialist Firearms (CTSF), **Armed Response Vehicle** (ARV) and Tactical Support Team (TST) units.

special operations (SO)

Operations that demand unique tactical techniques, methods of engagement and employment as well as equipment and training, and are often conducted in hostile, restricted or politically **sensitive** environments. Special operations, often referred to as special ops, are usually at least of the following: time-sensitive, **clandestine**, conducted with and/or through indigenous forces, conducted in low visibility including at night, requiring regional expertise and/or a high degree of risk. They can include **reconnaissance**, **psychological warfare** operations, **counterterrorism**, humanitarian assistance and hostage search and rescue. Unsurprisingly, it is often special forces that conduct special ops.

spice

Spice is a **synthetic** cannabinoid which some people consider worse than **heroin**. Although some people call it 'fake weed' because its mixture of shredded herbs and synthetic chemicals is similar to **cannabis**, its effects are very different and much stronger. Spice is often sold as incense or some kind of natural product, but it is dangerous and its use can, in some instances, be fatal. It can act as a relaxant, but it can also cause paranoia, aggression and violent behaviour. Spice is highly **addictive** and has spread rapidly through the UK's homeless population, being both cheap and strong, although its strength can vary widely.

Spice's street names include: black mamba, bliss, Bombay blue, fake weed, genie, K2, skunk, Yucatan fire and zohai.

S

spicer

Footpad, the lowest order of thieves (UK thieves' **cant**, historical slang).

spin

To search a **cell** (UK contemporary prison slang).

spinner

Handgun (UK contemporary slang).

splash

To stab (London contemporary gang slang associated with drill music).

spoke with

Robbed (UK thieves' **cant**, historical slang).

spoofing

Cybercriminals and **crackers** will often cover their tracks by spoofing or faking an IP address, or masking or changing the sender information on an email so as to deceive the recipient as to its origin. They can make an email appear as it if comes from a safe source, such as a trusted friend or well-known organisation so that you are more likely to click on the link it contains, which will then introduce **malware** in some way into your system, either by taking you to a site that injects it into your system or by directly injecting it so that crackers can access your computer and data.

spotter

Also known as an assessor. In **intelligence**, an **agent**, **asset** or **illegal** whose job it is to find and assess people in positions of value or potential value to an intelligence service.

spy

A spy can be an **intelligence officer** who works for a government **security service** or an **asset**, **agent** or foreign **source** who works for that service. Intelligence officers normally recruit and handle agents or assets who do the actual spying work and then send or deliver that information to their **handler** or **case officer**. The handler may have protective diplomatic status, also known as official **cover**, and be based in an embassy, or may have non-official cover. Spies can steal or gather military, governmental, economic and technical secrets, among others, or information that is of value to the nation state or security service that employs them. Spies can also carry out industrial **espionage**, sabotage or spread disinformation to the benefit of the country that employs them. Most countries spy on their allies as well as their enemies, although they do not officially admit to or comment on these operations. In addition, the security services and police **infiltrate** terrorist and other organisations to obtain information and possibly pre-empt attacks as well as protect national security. Spying, or espionage, is strictly controlled by law in most countries and there can be severe penalties, including expulsion and execution in some countries, if a spy is caught. ▶ **spy dust** Also known as *metka*, which is the Russian for 'mark', spy dust is a chemical marking compound composed of nitrophenyl pentadienal (NPPD) and **luminol**. It was developed and used by the KGB (now the FSB) to track a target foreign agent, officer or individual, who would unwittingly leave a trail once they had walked across or even

S

brushed against it. Spy dust was smeared on door knobs and sprinkled on the floors of apartments occupied by foreign persons of interest in Moscow and beyond. Its existence was only revealed to the West when a defecting agent informed American security services in 1984 and they got hold of a sample of it. ▶ **spy fiction** Spy fiction is a subgenre of the mystery and **thriller** genres. It focuses on **espionage** and usually features an agent or agents working for intelligence agencies. The James Bond series is perhaps the most famous example of spy fiction while John le Carré is considered to be one of the best exponents of the art. ▶ **spyware** Software designed to gather information about a user's computer use without their knowledge. Sometimes spyware is simply used to track a user's internet surfing habits for advertising purposes so it can then show you relevant ads. More dangerously, spyware can also scan computer files and keystrokes, create pop-up ads, change your homepage and/or redirect you to unsafe websites. A common scam is to generate a pop-up ad informing you that your system has been infected with a **virus** or some other form of **malware** and then force you to a webpage that has the solution to fix the problem. Most often, spyware is bundled with free software such as screen savers, emoticons and social networking programs.

S

SRAC
See **Short-Range Agent Communication**.

stabby
Protective stab vest worn by police officers (UK police slang).

stainless-steel ride

Prison term for death by **lethal** injection (US contemporary slang).

stalking

There is no strict official legal definition of 'stalking' in the UK, but it is an offence that can include acts such as following a person, watching or spying on them, or forcing contact with them through any means, including social media (see **cyber-stalking**). In many cases and when taken in isolation, the behaviour might appear innocent, but when carried out repeatedly so as to amount to a course of conduct, it may then cause significant alarm, harassment or distress to the victim. The effect on the victim is to curb their freedom and make them feel as if they constantly have to keep a watch out or look over their shoulder, and can be extremely distressing. Stalking has been known to escalate to other crimes of physical violence including murder.

staller

Pickpocket's **accomplice** whose job it was to keep up the arms of the victim (UK thieves' **cant**, historical slang).

starring the glaze

Smashing a pane of glass to facilitate a **robbery** (UK historical slang).

station

Overseas **Central Intelligence Agency** office or operational hub that is usually located in an official building such as an embassy. The officer in charge of it is known as the chief of station (COS).

statute of limitation

Legal time frame within which criminal **charges** must be filed against an **accused** or the **case** may no longer be prosecuted.

steel-jacketed bullet

Steel metallic envelope surrounding the core of a compound **bullet**.

steel shot

Soft steel **pellets** made specifically for use in **shotgun cartridges**.

steganography

The practice of hiding a digital file inside another, usually an image, so that, for example, a child pornography image can be hidden inside another graphic image file, audio file or other file format.

stick

Gun (London contemporary gang slang associated with drill music).

stimulant

Drug that immediately increases energy and alertness along with increases in blood pressure, heart rate and breathing.

stock

The part of a shoulder **firearm** which is held for firing and to which the **action** is attached. It is used to steady the firearm against the shoulder when firing.

stone

Bullet or **crack cocaine** (contemporary slang).

stop and search

A police officer can stop and search (S & S) someone in the UK if they have 'reasonable grounds' to suspect they are carrying **illegal drugs**, a weapon, stolen property or something which could be used to commit a crime. You can only be stopped and searched without reasonable grounds if it has been approved by a senior police officer. This can happen if it is suspected that serious violence could take place, the suspect is carrying a weapon or has used one, or they are in a specific location or area.

straight pull action

A **bolt-action** gun in which the bolt handle does not need to be rotated for locking and unlocking but can be handled by a straight backward and forward motion of the shooter's hand.

strap

Gun (UK contemporary slang). ▶ **strapped** Armed with a gun, carrying a gun (US contemporary gang slang).

strip

Area where **drugs** are sold (contemporary slang).

strychnine

Strychnine is a **poison** that was popular in the Victorian era as it was widely used in cities for pest control. Not the most subtle of poisons, strychnine causes frothing at the mouth followed by muscle spasms that grow so intense they asphyxiate the victim. The 1987 death of waxwork-museum owner Patsy Wright from cold medicine laced with strychnine remains unsolved, and in 1993 the Turkish president Turgut Özal was apparently assassinated by strychnine poisoning. Agatha Christie used strychnine as the murder method in several of her novels and short stories, as did Sir Arthur Conan Doyle and, more recently, Stephen King.

stun gun
Handheld contact weapon that uses a temporary high-voltage, low-current electrical **discharge** and delivers an electric shock that briefly disables, or stuns, the recipient.

sub-machine gun (SMG)
An **automatic firearm** that frequently **discharges pistol calibre ammunition** and is generally used with two hands.

succinylcholine (SUX)
Fast-acting **drug** that paralyses all the muscles in the body in less than a minute. It has no sedative effect, so the recipient remains fully awake. Succinylcholine has been suggested as an excellent murder weapon by the writer and pharmacist James J. Murray as it metabolises into two substances already present in the body: succinic acid and choline. The only slightly elevated levels of these found during an **autopsy** could therefore easily be overlooked unless there was other **evidence** indicating criminal activity.

S

summary offence

A summary offence is a less serious type of crime or offence that can be heard summarily by a magistrate or magistrates rather than a judge and jury. **Sentences** for summary offences are usually shorter and fines smaller than for more serious offences. Examples of summary offences include driving offences (not including death by dangerous driving), minor **criminal damage** and the lowest form of **assault** known as common assault. Summary offences exist within the common law jurisdictions of England, Scotland and Wales, Ireland, Canada, Australia, the US, Hong Kong, India, New Zealand, Malaysia and Singapore. In Canada they are known as summary conviction offences.

superintendent

There is a superintendent on call or working around the clock in most UK police forces. A police superintendent is responsible for a section of a borough or command, such as 'Operations', 'Crime' or 'Partnerships'. In some areas they are the local police commander for that designated area. They also carry a range of particular statutory authorities and act as senior public order or **firearms** commanders.

S

surveillance

Systematic **covert** or overt observation or monitoring of people, places, organisations or things by visual, aural, electronic, photographic or other means. To be effective, surveillance must go undetected. ▶ **surveillance detection** Measures taken to detect or determine if an individual, vehicle or location is under surveillance. A surveillance detection run (SDR) is an often-circuitous route taken by an officer or **case officer** to detect and flush out surveillance without alerting those who might be watching or monitoring them.

suspended sentence

When a prison term is not imposed if the defendant does not get into further trouble for the period they would have spent in jail or prison.

Suspicious Activity Report (SAR)

A Suspicious Activity Report alerts **law enforcement** in the UK and elsewhere to possible economic crime or terrorist financing. The reports are made by financial institutions and professionals such as accountants, solicitors and estate agents. They provide information from the private sector to law enforcement that would not otherwise be available and are vital in helping to tackle **money laundering**, **fraud** and other economic crimes. They also help to locate sex offenders, trace terrorist suspects, and detect and prevent organised and other serious crimes.

suttin

Meaning 'something' – a gun or a weapon (London contemporary gang slang associated with drill music).

SUX

See **succinylcholine**.

swag

Booty or plunder from a **robbery** or **burglary** (UK Victorian slang, contemporary slang).

swallow

A swallow was a female Russian **agent** or officer who was employed to seduce targets in **honey-trap** operations and effectively act as an **undercover** prostitute. The apartment in which she operated was known as a swallow's nest and was a double apartment where she would carry out her seduction in one room while the KGB recorded everything that happened from an adjoining room or apartment. Her male equivalent was known as a **raven**.

sweep

In **spy** lingo, to physically and/or electronically examine a room or area in order to detect any **clandestine** devices such as **bugs** or concealed electronic-listening devices.

swindler

A cheat or confidence artist who sets out to target and defraud honest tradesmen (UK thieves' **cant**, historical slang, also in contemporary use). In contemporary use, it is anyone who cheats another out of money or possessions. Elaborate scams are nothing new and even back in the sixteenth century gangs of swindlers were setting up stings, renting respectable houses in the most desirable parts of town and giving themselves the roles of 'masters, servants, porters, clerks, outriders and shopmen'. They then obtained credit through this show of opulence and proceeded to order goods, which they then sent to the countryside to be sold or bartered for other commodities. If they bartered for goods, these were then brought to London to be sold in turn.

S

Everything they bought was paid for with counterfeit money and their profit margins were huge on the goods they sold on. Once they had bled a town and its tradesmen dry, they moved on, swapping roles so that whoever had played the master now posed as a servant or outrider and so on. They also ran another scam where they would answer newspaper advertisements from distressed tradesmen looking for credit, promising to find them the money they needed once they had taken a deposit from them. Of course, those tradesmen never saw that deposit again or the promised loan, and were left in an even worse position. Many of them were then faced with ruin and the debtors' prison. These swindlers could be compared to the **grifters** in the United States and **con** artists and tricksters the world over who still practise today, although nowadays most often using the internet.

swing, swinging a line

Prisoners communicating from **cell** to cell, often by means of a piece of string which they swing from one cell to another (UK contemporary prison slang).

sword

A long, bladed weapon; also knife (London contemporary gang slang associated with drill music).

synthetic drug

Drug created artificially from chemicals, especially one made to resemble a natural product.

T

tak
Danish for 'thanks, thank you or please', and a word that
often occurs in **Scandi noir**.

take someone out of the box
To kill someone, usually a member of a rival gang (US
contemporary gang slang).

tartan noir
A genre of crime fiction set in Scotland and written by
Scottish writers or those based there, tartan noir has its
roots in the work of Robert Louis Stevenson and William
McIlvanney and was influenced by American **hard-boiled**
fiction writers such as Raymond Chandler and James
Ellroy. It is claimed that Ellroy coined the term when referring to Ian Rankin as 'the king of tartan noir' although
Rankin may have coined it himself when he asked Ellroy to
sign a book for him stating that he was a big fan and that he
wrote tartan noir. Rankin and Val McDermid spearheaded
this new wave of Scottish crime writing that now includes
multicultural elements but retains its overtones of cyni-
cism and a particularly world-weary point of view.

tax
To steal. Taxed – stolen (contemporary slang).

taxine

Unusual **poison** derived from yew tree seeds, berries, needles and leaves. It was used in Agatha Christie's *A Pocketful of Rye* (1953), where the victim is fed marmalade laced with taxine. Death is so rapid that the tell-tale signs of taxine poisoning – staggering, seizures, respiratory and heart failure – are often missed and it is only post-mortem that the cause of death is discovered.

tear up

A fight or to beat up (UK contemporary prison slang).

technical surveillance

Use of optical, audio or electronic monitoring or listening devices or systems, including vehicle trackers, to surreptitiously collect information.

teef

To steal (originally Jamaican slang, now in wider contemporary use).

teeth/teef

Bullets (London contemporary gang slang associated with drill music).

10-8

US police **code** that means an officer or unit is in service and available for calls. An officer will check on the radio or advise that they are ready for another call by 'taking a 10-8'. Officers may use it in conversation to describe a suspect who fled from them, saying the suspect 'got 10-8'.

10-4

US police **code** that means 'affirmative'. It can be used to answer 'yes' to a question or to advise that everything is OK.

10-13

US police **code** that refers to an officer's status or conditions. A dispatcher may ask an officer for their '10-13' to determine if everything is OK or if they need help; 10-13 can also refer to weather conditions, crowd issues or the status of a victim or suspect.

10-20

US police **code** that refers to the location of an officer or call. Some departments require their officers to provide their 10-20 whenever they initiate radio communications. Calls for service always include a 10-20, so the officer knows where to go.

TETRA

Terrestrial trunked radio, i.e. a two-way digital radio system, used for police communication (UK police acronym).

thallium

Agatha Christie used thallium in her 1961 novel *The Pale Horse*, with the narrative resting on the fact that it is a handy **poison** for a murder thanks to it being odourless and tasteless as well as easily blended with food and drink. Thallium is also highly detectable as it remains in body tissue for weeks. Although it was once widely available in rat poison, it is now tightly controlled. It was used in the 1991 murder of Robert Curley by his wife, Joann, in Pennsylvania and of a computer engineer named Xiaoye Wang in New Jersey in 2011, who was poisoned by his estranged wife Li. Thallium

T

was also the poison of choice for women in Sydney, Australia, in the 1950s. In 1952–3 there were a hundred thallium poisonings with ten deaths resulting from them. The majority of the perpetrators were female and the victims male. Investigators initially thought that Alexander Litvinenko, murdered in 2006 in London, had been poisoned with thallium as he had the classic flu-like symptoms, failing eyesight and his hair had fallen out, but the poison was later found to be **polonium**. The antidote for thallium is Prussian Blue which, ironically, is derived from **cyanide**.

THC

Tetrahydrocannabinol or THC is the main psychoactive constituent in **cannabis**.

theft

Theft is the act of stealing or of taking another person's property without their permission or consent with the intention of unlawfully depriving them of it. ▶ **thief** A thief is someone who acts by stealth to steal or take another person's property without their permission or consent and with the intention of unlawfully depriving them of it.

thriller

The thriller genre is wide-ranging and can best be characterised by the emotions it evokes including excitement, anticipation, fascination, fear and tension. Suspense is a crucial element along with action and uncertainty. A good thriller keeps its audience on the edge of their seats, either literally or metaphorically, until the final act or denouement. There are multiple subgenres including action thrillers, **spy fiction**, **psychological thrillers**, romantic thrillers, historical thrillers, political thrillers and **courtroom**

dramas. The thriller genre encompasses books, films and television.

TIC

Taken Into Consideration (UK police acronym).

time bomb

When related to **cybercrime**, a time bomb is a malicious program designed to execute at a predetermined time and/or date. Time bombs are often set to trigger on special days such as national holidays or on anniversaries of global events to make a political statement. When it executes, a time bomb can do something innocuous such as displaying a particular image, but it can also do something far more damaging such as stealing, deleting or corrupting system information. The time bomb remains dormant until the pre-set trigger time arrives.

tool

Gun; to be 'tooled up' is to be equipped with a weapon, especially a gun (contemporary slang).

tooling

Pickpocketing using an implement or tool to open the pocket (UK historical slang).

T

topping

Execution by hanging. ▶**topping cheat** Gallows. ▶**topping cove** Hangman (UK thieves' **cant**, historical slang).

toss

In **tradecraft**, placing a drop, or passing on an item, by throwing it while on the move by foot or by vehicle (see **car toss**).

total metal jacket

Projectile in which the **bullet** jacket encloses the whole core, including the base. (See **full metal jacket**.)

touch

To **arrest** (UK thieves' **cant**, historical slang).

toxic

Harmful, destructive, deadly or **poisonous** to a living organism. ▶**toxicity** Degree or level to which a substance is **poisonous** or can harm somebody or something.

toy

Depending on the context can refer to a gun, car, **drugs** or item of drug paraphernalia (UK contemporary slang).

trace evidence

Trace **evidence** is created when objects make contact and is often transferred by heat or created by contact friction. Dr Edmond Locard demonstrated the importance of trace evidence with the formulation of **Locard's Exchange Principle**. **Forensic** scientists use trace evidence to reconstruct crimes as well as in accident **investigation** to establish what happened. Examples of trace evidence include **gunshot residue**, blood, **fingerprints** and fibres as well impressions such as **bullet** holes and bitemarks. Trace evidence is vulnerable to **contamination** and the scene must therefore be preserved and the evidence collected following established procedures and guidelines.

T

tradecraft

Operational and particular methods, techniques, skills and equipment used in the organisation and performance of **intelligence** services and activities, especially techniques and methods for handling communications with **agents** such as **dead drops**.

transcript

Official written record of everything that was said at a court proceeding, a hearing or a deposition.

transfer bloodstain

This is when a bloodied surface comes into contact with another surface and some of the blood is then transferred to that new surface. Transfer **bloodstains** can be especially useful in establishing the sequence of events and also raise the possibility of **fingerprint** and other **trace evidence** in the bloodstains.

transportation

Transportation was an alternative to hanging as a punishment in seventeenth- to nineteenth-century England, initially being used when death was considered too severe a penalty and later as an alternative for what had previously been capital crimes. It was a cheaper way than prison to remove a criminal from society as the only cost was that of the passage. As well as convicts, transportees included political prisoners, debtors and prisoners-of-war from Ireland and Scotland. The Transportation Act of 1717 permitted the courts to **sentence** prisoners to seven years' transportation to America. Although seven years was the usual term, sometimes the sentence was for life. If they were

T

freed after seven years, they had to make their own way back home and usually could not afford to do so, staying on in the colonies to work and therefore act as some of the first settlers in Australia.

Prisoners were sent to the Americas from 1610 until the American Revolution in 1776, when transportation was suspended by the Criminal Law Act. The first transportations to Australia started in 1787 and continued until 1868. Around 162,000 men, women and children were transported to Australia, some as young as nine years old. Estimates of the numbers transported to America vary between 50,000 and 120,000. Alternative transportation destinations included Bermuda and, unsuccessfully, to Ghana and Senegal. Other countries that practised transportation include the then Soviet Union and France, most notoriously sending the army officer Alfred Dreyfus, wrongly convicted of treason in 1894, to its penal colony on Devil's Island in a case that became known as the Dreyfus Affair.

trap-and-trace device
Device that captures incoming electronic or other impulses that identify the source of a wire or electronic communication.

T

trapp
Constable or person who apprehends thieves (UK thieves' **cant**, historical slang).

trash cover
Federal Bureau of Investigation term for an intentional search of a specific person's rubbish at their home or business

in an effort to find information relevant to an ongoing **investigation** when 'no reasonable expectation of privacy exists'.

tray eight
.38 **calibre handgun** (US contemporary gang slang).

tree jumper
Rapist of women (US contemporary gang slang).

Trident
Police from Operation Trident, the **Metropolitan Police** gang division (London contemporary gang slang associated with drill music).

trigger
Part of a **firearm**'s mechanism, which is squeezed or pressed by the finger to cause the firearm to **discharge**.
▶ **trigger guard** Loop that partially surrounds the trigger to reduce the possibility of accidental **discharge**.

trip
Common name for the **hallucinogenic** experience produced by taking a **drug** such as **lysergic acid diethylamide** (LSD) or **ketamine**. If someone takes enough ketamine that they completely dissociate and are unable to feel or experience the world around them, then this is colloquially known as 'falling into a k-hole'.

T

triple agent
Agent who serves three **intelligence** services but who, like a **double agent**, knowingly or unknowingly withholds significant information from two services at the instigation of the third service.

Trojan

In relation to **cybercrime**, a Trojan, or Trojan Horse, is a malicious program disguised to look like a valid program. This makes it difficult to distinguish from programs that are supposed to be on a system. Once introduced, a Trojan can change information, steal passwords, destroy files and carry out any other illicit task for which it was designed. It may also remain dormant until a **cracker** accesses it remotely to take control of the system. A Trojan is very similar to a **virus** but cannot replicate.

trophy

Many serial killers collect a trophy or souvenir from their victims or **crime scenes**. This can include clothing, jewellery or an actual body part. **Ed Gein**, on whom both *Psycho* (1960) and *The Silence of the Lambs* (1991) are based, turned body parts from his victims into household items including bowls created from skulls and a wastebasket from human skin as well as masks from human faces. **Ted Bundy** displayed his victims' heads in his apartment while **Jeffrey Dahmer** kept his victims' genitals in a lobster pot. The Ukrainian serial killer Anatoly Onoprienko kept underwear from all his female victims and even gave some of it to his then girlfriend. Killers who keep trophies such as jewellery will often give it to a family member or close friend. Others like to take out a trophy or look at it to enable them to relive the crime and the satisfaction, including sexual satisfaction, they gained from it. Trophies are not confined to serial killers – the 'Shoe Rapist' James Lloyd took pairs of shoes from his victims. He was convicted of four **rapes** and two **attempted** rapes, but police believe the figure was much higher as 126 pairs of shoes were found in his possession after his **arrest**.

T

tuck-up fair

Gallows (UK Victorian slang).

tug

The police stopping someone: 'I gave him a tug.' It can also mean a police officer being taking to one side by a senior officer for a minor **misdemeanour** (UK contemporary police slang).

turnover

Official term for the handing of an **intelligence agent** from one **case officer** to a new one, i.e. turning them over to another.

turtles

Short for turtle doves or gloves, a necessary accoutrement for every professional criminal to avoid **forensic** detection (UK cockney rhyming slang).

two

'A two' is a two-year **sentence**. Similarly 'a four' is a four-year sentence, 'an eight' is an eight-year sentence, etc. (UK contemporary prison slang).

TWOC

'Taking Without Owner's Consent' (UK police acronym).

201 file

File that contains the personal or 'personality' information of a **Central Intelligence Agency** operative. It can also refer to a US military personnel file.

U

UCO
Undercover officer (UK police acronym).

UMBRAGE
Central Intelligence Agency's **hacking** group, part of its Remote Development Branch, that allegedly stores hacking signatures and techniques stolen from other nation states, including the Russian Federation. They then allegedly use these signatures or 'fingerprints' during their own attacks to misdirect and make it appear as if they emanate from elsewhere, according to Wikileaks.

unauthorised disclosure
Communication, leaking or physical transfer of **classified**, or unclassified but **sensitive**, information to an unauthorised recipient, including the media.

unconditional discharge
Sentence in a criminal **case** in which the defendant is released without imprisonment, **probation** supervision or conditions.

undeclared
Intelligence officer, **asset**, **agent** or action whose affiliation to an intelligence service or **agency** is not formally identified to a **foreign intelligence** or **security service**, government, organisation or other entity.

undercover

Covert, **clandestine** or secret work, especially by the police or for **espionage** purposes, is known as 'undercover' and is normally carried out by officers or **agents** in plain clothes or disguise who try to blend in with the community or organisation they are investigating or **infiltrating**.

undy

Undercover police officer (London contemporary slang).

unilateral operation

Clandestine or secret operation or activity conducted without the knowledge or assistance of a **foreign intelligence** or **security service**, host country, foreign organisation or other entity.

United Nations Office on Drugs and Crime

The United Nations Office on Drugs and Crime (UNODC) helps member states fight **illegal drugs**, crime and terrorism, and operates throughout the world in an extensive network of field offices.

United States Secret Service (USSS)

Federal **law enforcement agency** mandated by US Congress to carry out the dual missions of the protection of national and visiting foreign leaders and criminal **investigations**.

unknown subject (unsub)

The subject of a criminal **investigation** whose identity has not been determined is commonly referred to as an 'unsub'.

up on it

Successful **drug dealer** or someone who has a lot of knowledge about drugs (US contemporary gang slang).

V

validation

In **intelligence** terms, the process that confirms that the need to collect or produce a particular piece of intelligence is sufficiently important to justify the dedication of intelligence resources, does not duplicate an existing requirement, and has not been previously satisfied.

vanilla

Judge. Derived from rhyming slang, vanilla fudge – judge (UK contemporary prison slang).

vehicle-borne improvised explosive device (VBIED)

Formal technical term for a car bomb.

VENONA

The top-secret US codebreaking operation during the Second World War that deciphered Soviet **intelligence** messages transmitted between Moscow and other cities concerning US **spy** and other activities was known as the VENONA project. From the traffic, the Americans discovered that the Soviets had over three hundred **assets** of various kinds inside numerous US government agencies.

V

Vera

Cigarette paper. Derived from rhyming slang, Vera Lynn
– skin (UK contemporary prison slang).

Violent Criminal Apprehension Program (ViCAP)

An **Federal Bureau of Investigation** programme that
maintains a nationwide data information centre to collect,
collate and analyse violent crimes. ViCAP **analysts** examine crime data and patterns to identify potential similari-
ties between crimes, and identify homicide and **sexual
assault** trends and patterns.

virus

A computer virus is a malicious program or **code** that
attaches itself to another program file where it can replicate
itself and then infect other systems. A computer virus
spreads from one system to another when the infected
program is used by the other system. It can therefore spread
rapidly and easily on networked systems and can also be
transmitted via other media such as a CD or memory stick.
It can also be emailed with an attachment. A virus is different from other **malware** such as adware and **Trojans** in
that it can self-replicate.

visit

To leave prison for some purpose, e.g. 'I'm going on a visit'
(UK contemporary prison slang).

volunteer

In **intelligence** terms, someone who initiates contact
voluntarily to offer information or services to an intelligence service or government, whether by calling, writing or

walking in to an embassy or other government office, often in return for political asylum, out of greed or a desire for revenge. Also known as a walk-in.

VX

VX (O-ethyl S-diisopropylaminomethyl methylphosphono-thiolate) is a liquid **nerve agent** that is entirely manufactured in the UK. It is tasteless, colourless, odourless and a hundred times more potent than **sarin**, penetrating the skin and causing paralysis that leads to rapid respiratory failure. VX is classified by the United Nations as a **weapon of mass destruction**. In February 2017 it was used to kill Kim Jong-nam, the half-brother of North Korean leader Kim Jong-un, at Kuala Lumpur airport.

V

W

wadding
Plastic or fibre filler **loaded** in **shotgun cartridges** to isolate propellant from **pellets**.

walk-in
See **volunteer**.

wap
Gun (London contemporary gang slang associated with drill music).

wardriving
Wardriving is the act of driving around in a vehicle to find an open, unsecured wi-fi network that will then be added to a map of exploitable zones to be used at a later date or passed on to others. The range of a wireless network will often go beyond the bounds of the building it covers, creating public zones that can be exploited to gain entry to the network and carry out **cybercrime**.

weapon of mass destruction (WMD)
Chemical, biological, radiological or nuclear weapon capable of creating widespread damage or destruction, and of causing mass casualties.

wet up
To cut up another prisoner (UK contemporary prison slang).

whack up

To beat up (UK contemporary prison slang).

White List

The identities and locations of people who have been identified as being of **intelligence** or **counterintelligence** interest and are expected to be able to provide information or assistance in existing or new intelligence areas of interest. (See also **Black List** and **Grey List**.)

whodunnit

Often interchangeable with the detective fiction and **cosy mystery** genres of crime fiction, the whodunnit focuses on deducing who committed a crime, usually a murder, by solving a series of clues. There are traditionally lots of plot twists and red herrings to confuse the reader before the protagonist is exposed in the denouement.

window of detection

Time period within which a **drug** can be detected in a biological sample such as urine.

wiseguy

Made man, someone who is a member of the US **Mafia**.

WMD

See **weapon of mass destruction**.

woosh

To shoot (London contemporary gang slang associated with drill music).

worm

A worm is very similar to a computer **virus** as it is a
destructive, self-contained program that can replicate
itself and is therefore favoured by cybercriminals.
Unlike a virus, a worm does not need to be a part of
another program or document. A worm can copy and
transfer itself to other systems on a network without
any kind of user intervention and can prove devastating
if not isolated and removed. A worm replicating out of
control can consume system resources such as memory
and bandwidth until a system becomes unstable, and
can cause an enormous amount of damage.

wrap-up

Restrain or confine a prisoner in their **cell** before moving
them (UK contemporary prison slang).

written statement

Permanent, written record of the pre-trial testimony of the
accused, suspects, victims, **complaints** and witnesses.

wrong-un

Paedophile (UK contemporary prison slang).

Wuornos, Aileen

Aileen Wuornos (1956–2002) was that rare thing: a
female serial killer. The survivor of an abusive and horrify-
ingly chaotic childhood, Wuornos was born in Michigan in
the US to a father who killed himself while in prison for

child molestation and a mother who abandoned her young family. Raised by her grandparents, Aileen was sexually abused by her grandfather and had sexual relations with her brother, giving up a baby for adoption in her early teens. She lived as a vagabond in adulthood, hitchhiking and earning money as a sex worker.

Briefly married, Wuornos already had a long criminal history by the time she met Tyria Moore in 1986 in Florida and began a relationship with her. From 1989, when the body of Richard Mallory was found in a junkyard, until 1991, Wuornos murdered at least six men along the Florida highways where she plied her trade as a sex worker, shooting all of them. Moore and Wuornos were traced through palm and **fingerprints** left in the crashed car of another missing man and Moore did a deal with prosecutors, getting Wuornos to confess to all the murders over a taped phone conversation.

Wuornos claimed she had killed Mallory in self-defence as he had **raped** her, and it later turned out that he had served ten years in prison for **sexual assault**, although this was not revealed in court. Wuornos also claimed the other five killings were in self-defence, although she later retracted this. She was given the death penalty for all six killings, spent ten years on death row and was executed by **lethal** injection in 2002 when Governor of Florida Jeb Bush lifted a temporary stay of execution and a team of psychiatrists deemed her mentally competent, even though at least one state-appointed attorney expressed severe doubts about her mental state. Wuornos is the subject of several documentaries and was depicted by Charlize Theron in the film *Monster* (2003), for which Theron won an Academy Award.

X

X-Files, The

The X-Files was a long-running science-fiction TV series focusing on the activities of two **Federal Bureau of Investigation special agents**, Fox Mulder and Dana Scully, played by David Duchovny and Gillian Anderson respectively. The series ran from 1993 to 2018 and focused on **investigations** into paranormal activity, with Mulder a strong believer in the supernatural while Scully remained sceptical until she became a reluctant believer, explaining away the paranormal with science. Some episodes were based on real-life events; both the US and the UK, along with other global powers including Russia, run military and **intelligence** programs that investigate, or have investigated, paranormal events and suspected activity.

XO

Executive officer, the second in command of a military unit in the US.

X-ray

X-rays are used to identify human remains, among other **forensic** uses, usually of the spine, upper leg or skull. A side X-ray of the skull can be used to identify a body with 97 per cent certainty while cervical, or neck, vertebrae provide a greater than 98 per cent accuracy. An X-ray can also be used to display and locate any foreign objects in a body such as a **bullet** and to help detect various traumatic and pathological changes. It can help identify sharp-force injuries and the weapon used, as well as being helpful in motor-vehicle related deaths. X-rays are also helpful for complex injury evaluation in victims where abuse is suspected. ▶ **X-ray fluorescence (XRF) spectroscopy** Non-destructive analytical technique that uses X-rays for elemental analysis and is particularly useful in **forensic** science. Compared to other forensic techniques it is fast, often giving results within minutes, and portable XRF machines can be taken to **crime scenes** to analyse and produce results on the spot. XRF is used to analyse rock, soils, paints, inks, **gunshot residue** and even counterfeit coins.

Y

yardie

Member of a Jamaican gang, or a gang mostly composed of Jamaicans, involved in the **drugs** trade and prone to torture and extreme violence. Can also be used by Jamaicans to refer to a fellow Jamaican (UK/Jamaican contemporary slang).

yeng

Gun (US/Jamaican contemporary gang slang).

YOI

See **Young Offender Institution**.

You all right/you want anything?

Used by **drug dealers** to ask someone if they want any drugs (UK/US contemporary gang slang).

Young Offender Institution (YOI)

UK prison that houses prisoners aged eighteen to twenty-one.

youth custody

Establishments that house young people in the UK under the age of eighteen who have been remanded in **custody** or **sentenced** to periods of detention by the courts.

Z

zero day

A zero-day vulnerability is one that is as yet unknown to the creators of the software, and is potentially exploitable thanks to that security hole or vulnerability. It is also as yet unknown to antivirus or anti-malware vendors. A zero-day exploit is the **code** that **hackers** use to exploit this hole. The term 'zero day' refers to the number of days the owner of the software has known about the vulnerability. Zero-day exploits and codes are extremely valuable, and a thriving market has grown to trade them, largely fuelled by government **intelligence** agencies. Some infamous programs that employed zero-day exploits include Stuxnet, a **virus** that attacked Iran's Natanz uranium enrichment plant, and Operation Aurora, an attack by what are believed to be Chinese hackers who broke into the systems of Google, Adobe and a dozen other companies. The **Central Intelligence Agency** allegedly uses zero-day exploits in **malware** that can penetrate and infest both the Android phone and iPhone software that runs or has run presidential Twitter accounts. Of course, this means that as long as they conceal this vulnerability from Google and Apple, these phones remain hackable by the CIA.

Zodiac Killer

The Zodiac Killer is the name given to the as yet unidentified serial killer who carried out murders in Northern California from the late 1960s or earlier until the early 1970s. The name 'Zodiac' came from a series of letters sent by someone, assumed to be male, claiming to be the perpetrator to the Bay Area press. The letters contained four cryptograms, only one of which has been solved to date. There are so far seven confirmed victims of the Zodiac Killer, two of whom survived, with another possible twenty-eight, although the killer himself claimed thirty-seven. There have been a number of theories and claims as to the true identity of the killer and in 2018 the Vallejo police department submitted the envelopes he used in his correspondence for **DNA** testing but have never released the results to the public.

zombie, zombie drone

A zombie is a **malware** program that can be used by a cybercriminal to remotely take control of a system. It can then be used as a zombie drone for further attacks, such as denial-of-service (DoS) attacks, without a user's knowledge. Zombies can be introduced to a system by simply opening an infected email attachment, but are also often inadvertently downloaded through file-sharing sites, chat groups, adult websites and online casinos that force you to download their media player to have access to the content on their site and then use the installed player as the delivery mechanism for the zombie.

Z

zoning

Surveillance technique in which the surveillance area is divided into zones, with surveillants assigned to cover a specific zone or area.

Acknowledgements

This book came about thanks to the launch of another book, serendipity and a couple of glasses of wine. That other book was Jonathon Green's *The Stories of Slang* and those glasses of wine unleashed a torrent of ideas that I decided to share with his editor, Duncan Proudfoot, one of which was a dictionary of crime. He loved it, told me I should write it and then convinced me I actually could. Two years later, I handed him the completed manuscript. It marked not just a new departure for me but my return to being published after a prolonged period caring for a seriously ill family member. I am forever grateful to Duncan, a gentleman as well as a fine editor, for believing in me and for opening the door once again to a world I love.

I am also grateful to Lisa Moylett, my astounding, indefatigable agent who nurtures her authors while eating LA lawyers for breakfast, and to Jamie Maclean, Zoe Apostolides and Elena Langtry who make up the rest of the hotbed of creativity that is CMM. You all not only rock but you are some of the most genuinely wonderful people I know.

Of course, I must thank Jonathon Green because without him this book would never have happened, and the other authors at CMM who are so mutually supportive. I'm also grateful for Jonathon's occasional prod on Twitter when I get something wrong and even when I get something right.

Thanks also to the team at Little, Brown who have shaped this book, especially the eagle-eyed Howard Watson who copy edits with precision and flair, and Rebecca Sheppard who calmly and efficiently pulls everything together. I am writing this months before the book is launched but I know you will do that brilliantly too.

One of my oldest friends, Sean Lashley, was a serving officer with the Metropolitan Police Service for many years and helped me out with acronyms and police slang, much of which I heard from him as he recounted tales of what had gone on at the nick. Huge thanks too to my other sources whom I cannot name but who were immensely helpful. You know who you are and you all do a fine job.

Finally, my heartfelt gratitude to my friends, family and fellow writers, often interchangeable, who have been there for me through good times and bad. There are too many of you to name but, again, you know who you are and I love you all equally. Except maybe my daughter. I might love her a little bit more.